MAGICAL MAY

A practical guide to living an inspired life

FLAVIA WAAS

BALBOA
PRESS

A DIVISION OF HAY HOUSE

Balboa Press books may be ordered through booksellers or by contacting:

Balboa Press
A Division of Hay House
1663 Liberty Drive
Bloomington, IN 47403
www.balboapress.com.au
1 (877) 407-4847

Because of the dynamic nature of the Internet, any web addresses or
links contained in this book may have changed since publication and
may no longer be valid. The views expressed in this work are solely those
of the author and do not necessarily reflect the views of the publisher,
and the publisher hereby disclaims any responsibility for them.

The author of this book does not dispense medical advice or prescribe the use
of any technique as a form of treatment for physical, emotional, or medical
problems without the advice of a physician, either directly or indirectly. The
intent of the author is only to offer information of a general nature to help
you in your quest for emotional and spiritual well-being. In the event you use
any of the information in this book for yourself, which is your constitutional
right, the author and the publisher assume no responsibility for your actions.

Any people depicted in stock imagery provided by Thinkstock are models,
and such images are being used for illustrative purposes only.
Certain stock imagery © Thinkstock.

Print information available on the last page.

ISBN: 978-1-5043-0623-2 (sc)
ISBN: 978-1-5043-0624-9 (e)

Balboa Press rev. date: 01/24/2017

Dedication

To all you fellow dreamers

Introduction

At the beginning of 2016 a lot happened for me. It started off with my partner and I buying land, something we've both been wanting for so long. A month later my brother visited and I got engaged to Andy. We visited my fiancées parents in the following month and after we got back from New Zealand, where they live, we got married. Then my parents arrived and stayed for 3 weeks. And, I almost forgot to mention, we also started building a house!

On top of all that, I continued doing my work for my clients, managed to keep up with my yoga and meditation practice - maybe I missed a few days or weeks, oops! I caught up with friends, went for walks, did my tax return, and lots more. It wasn't stressful, it was actually very enjoyable. But I can't tell you how much I was looking forward to more time and less things to do. I wondered what I would be doing with all that extra time and decided that I'd be working on manifesting my dreams. I would dedicate the whole month of May to it.

And I did. Each day for 31 days I focused on something that I wanted to bring into my life. Each day I made sure to think only positive, empowering thoughts and cultivate an attitude of "anything is possible". I uncovered negative, restricting beliefs and replaced them with positive beliefs of abundance, joy and love.

And I shared my daily exercises with anyone who was interested on my blog and my Facebook page. And this is how "Magical May" was born.

Read this book anytime, it doesn't matter whether it's May or June or December. "Magical May" applies to any month of the year. You don't have to start on the 1st of a month either, start whenever you feel ready. You can read a chapter each day or every two days. You can also read the whole book in one day and go back to individual chapters and exercises later. If you do choose to read one chapter per day, I'd recommend you to start day 1 on a Sunday since this was when the original "Magical May" started. How you use this book is entirely up to you. I hope it'll be as helpful to you as it was to me. I've enjoyed writing it so much, I hope you'll enjoy reading it just as much.

Chapter 1

How to Prepare...

"Those who don't believe in magic will never find it."

– Roald Dahl

The first task I'd like to give you to prepare for "Magical May", is to think about how you'd like the following 31 days to be. Then repeat to yourself: "The next 31 days will be full of magic." Or maybe even "The next 31 days will be the most magical days of my life so far!" Be creative. Say it to yourself until you feel excited about the magical experiences that await you in "Magical May". You could even go further and write a vision for this coming month. I didn't take the time to write a vision before I started but if I had, it would have sounded something like this:

"This coming month is full of magic. Each day I wake up feeling grateful for all the good things that I have in my life. Each day I take time to be present and observe my surroundings. I sit in stillness and empty my mind. I become more aware of my own inner guidance and take time to listen to the messages I'm receiving. I'm monitoring my thoughts very carefully and changing any negative thought patterns and beliefs. I'm becoming very clear about what it is that I'd like to create and take all the necessary steps towards receiving it. I'm choosing wisely where I put my energy, knowing that whatever I put my attention to I create more of. I'm dedicated and committed to making the next 31 days the most magical and joyful days of my life."

How did it feel to write down your vision? It's nice to be clear about something, isn't it? I wish I had done this before every month of my life but a lot of the time I just waited for what life threw at me and then reacted to it. Only when I realized that life's not happening to me but I'm creating my experiences did I make the effort to putting thought into how I wanted my life to be like.

The other thing I'd recommend you to do in order to prepare for "Magical May" is, do some cleaning. Or do you want to manifest your dreams from a place of chaos, stagnation, dust, neglect and dirt? I don't know about you but I can't do work on my computer unless my desk is clean. And I can't do work on manifesting amazing things unless my place feels amazing! Take as much time as you need, a day, 2 days or a week. Make your space look and feel beautiful so that when you start day 1 of "Magical May" you can sit down to meditate in your spotless home and think to yourself "I love my home". Not: "I should do some cleaning". I personally really like cleaning and I can tell you why – I wrote a whole article about cleaning once. And here are some of the highlights:

Why I love cleaning? Because I love the end result of my house being clean. And I have to admit, I even like the process of cleaning. If you don't enjoy cleaning at all, maybe I can convince you to do so. There are a lot of benefits in giving your house a good clean and now's a good time.

#1 Your outer world is reflecting your inner world

My co-workers in various jobs have commented on my spotless desk, "wow, so clean." Their desks were all cluttered and dusty and just looking at their chaos made me feel stressed. I tried to find an explanation for my clean desk and this is why I was keeping my working space "zen" as my friend would say: If there's chaos on my desk, there's chaos in my mind. And the other way round, if there's chaos in my mind, there's chaos on my desk. So before I start working, my desk needs to be clean. I'm more focused and less distracted. I get work done faster too. And it's the same with my home, I feel so unbalanced when the place is a mess. I remember getting back home from Hawaii last year. I spent the whole day cleaning, rearranging and decorating. Then I stopped, looked at my fresh, new place and smiled. Not only was my house clean again, I felt like I had done a cleansing of my body, mind and soul.

#2 Paying attention to the dark and dusty corners

The other thing I noticed when cleaning was that I didn't always clean everywhere. I tended to avoid the dark corners or top shelves or any other places that were a bit harder to access. I was aware of it but still, I didn't feel like getting into it. And again, I tried to relate the process of cleaning to myself. Was I avoiding the dark corners of my soul? Often we hold on to old hurts and pains and fears and we don't want to look at them because it brings up these feelings again. So knowing that I'd feel much better when I did look at them, work through them and then let them go, I started dusting off those top shelves.

#3 We are what we own?

Sometimes I clean but something's still not right. And in most cases, it's the kind of stuff I surround myself with or the amount of stuff I surround myself with. Just look around you and analyse your "stuff situation". If you've arranged the books on the shelves and dusted them off and you're still not satisfied, maybe they're a) the wrong books and/or b) too many of them? I go through all my stuff from time to time and re-asses. My clothes, my books, any other stuff I own. Some things are easy to let go of, they go straight onto the "no" pile. Others I'm not sure about, that's the "maybe" pile and some of my things I definitely want to keep. Usually the "maybe" pile's the biggest. I ask myself, when did I wear this last? Or did I ever wear it? If not, it goes onto the "no" pile. No going back, no reconsidering. And then I make sure to move the stuff out of my home quickly. And that doesn't mean moving it into the shed or garage "for a while". I do a garage sale, take stuff to Vinnies, Salvos or the used book store, give it to a friend in need or sell it on gumtree or ebay - the sooner the better.

#4 Redecorating

Another thing I did as part of my last spring cleaning was to rearrange a few things. I got rid of what I didn't need anymore and the place looked and felt clean and tidy. But I still wasn't satisfied. Again I looked at myself and I realised that I had changed. My priorities had changed, some of my beliefs had changed, my attitude had changed. I felt the need to adjust my outer world to reflect the changes within me. So I started moving around furniture and rugs, putting up new candles and fabrics and rearranging picture frames differently. I had bought a few little things in Hawaii that I hung up on the walls or set up on tables and shelves. And we had been to IKEA on the way home so I had lots of new things to work with. I was happy again, for now. Until the next big change.

Did the article inspire you and convince you that cleaning is awesome? I hope you're enjoying your "cleaning journey" very much.

DAY
1

"The words you speak become the house you live in."

—Hafiz

Good morning everyone! Welcome to "Magical May". And what were your first thoughts this morning? Mine were "another beautiful day" and "ah, it's Sunday!" and "I'm looking forward to creating some magic". Something along those lines. I used to have the mantra "today's the best day of my life" and I would say it every day first thing in the morning. Why did I do this? Because our thoughts create our reality. So you better think good thoughts and start the day with a positive statement. What were your thoughts this morning?

Exercise 1: watch your thoughts. Not just in the morning, throughout the whole day. If they're negative, if you worry, stress, push, get impatient, tell yourself that it's all perfect and repeat to yourself that this day is the best day ever and that everything will work out perfectly well.

This exercise is something you'll want to integrate into your life and make it a habit. And if this is very new to you, go to YouTube and type in "Your Words and Thoughts Create Your World!" by one of my favourite authors and spiritual teachers Louise Hay.

And there's something else I did this morning and I encourage you to do this every morning from today on. At least try to do it for the next 31 days: give thanks.

Exercise 2: every morning, write down 10 things you're grateful for. Because it's like Louise Hay says, the universe loves gratitude! And the more grateful we are for what we have, the more things we'll receive to be grateful for.

"I'm so grateful for the rain because it fills our water tank and feeds the plants."

"I'm so grateful for my car because it's so reliable."

"I'm so grateful for my home because it makes me feel safe."

"I'm so grateful for my friends because they make me laugh."

"I'm so grateful for my health because I'm able to live a life without restrictions."

And so on.

DAY 2

"Start each day with a grateful heart."

Good morning everyone, happy Monday. Are you sad that the weekend is over or do you choose to be happy on a Monday too? You may go to work and maybe you don't want to sit in the office the whole day. But hey, there are a lot of good things about going to work. The most obvious one is, you earn money. That money paid for your breakfast this morning and it's paying for your rent as well. It's also paying for your next trip overseas, your car and your clothes. So this morning, be grateful for your work, because it sustains you. And if you'd like to have another job, put it on your wish list! And this is what we're going to do today, we're making a list of all the things we want to manifest in our lives. But first things first.

Exercise 1: Write down 10 things you're grateful for today and why.

And how are you going with the positive thinking? I caught myself going into a negative pattern yesterday but since I was watching my thoughts, I was able to pull myself out and turn it around again. I've been practicing for years so don't worry if you don't master it after a day or two. Now to the fun part, our wish list.

Exercise 2: Write a list of all the things you want to attract into your life. This can be material things like a house, a car, designer jeans, a new bikini, a flight ticket to Tahiti and a dehumidifier (that's what I've got on my list. Not very sexy but I really need one!). Include people on your list as well, like a soul mate, good friends, and a supportive boss. Or improving relationships you already have with your current partner, work colleagues, house mates. You can also include experiences you'd like to have, like hiking in the Himalayas, surfing big waves, riding horses through Mongolia. And you can write down feelings as well. Feeling at peace, being more confident, being fulfilled, feeling loved, joyful, happy and energised.

Don't just write down the big things, big things sometimes take longer. If you want to build a house it won't happen in a day. So add a few smaller things too, just to practice. Like a parking spot every time you go into town. My mum has mastered the parking spots. She always parks in the same section (section P). It can be very satisfying to see magic working on a smaller scale. And then we can work ourselves up to the dream houses and private jets.

Also, explore the "why" behind your wishes. Why do you want to have a new car, a bigger house or a boyfriend/girlfriend? You don't need to come up with a rational, logical answer for this one. It can be enough to simply say, "I want a boyfriend because I love hugs and I love waking up next to someone." Asking yourself why you want something brings you closer to the feeling you'll feel once you've received the car, the boyfriend, the hiking experience or feeling peaceful. And feeling it is one of the keys to manifesting your desires. There's a great video by Abraham Hicks on YouTube. Just search for "Abraham Hicks -- Secret to Manifest Your Desire".

For today, let's just write our list and explore why we want something. Try to feel how it feels to have it. And be clear about what you want. Don't make a compromise like, "but I'd also be happy with a smaller car". So do you not want the big car? Do you want a small car instead? What do you want? How can the universe reply to your vague description of a car? Making compromises also means you don't believe that you can have what you want. But we'll talk about this on another day.

Have fun!

DAY

3

"The size of your dreams must always exceed your current capacity to achieve them. If your dreams do not scare you, they are not big enough."

—Ellen Johnson Sirleaf

How did it feel to write your list? Is it a long list or a short list? Did you ask for a lot or only a little? When I look at my list, it's full of amazing things. But none of them are over the top and I wonder why I didn't allow myself to dream a little bigger? One of the things I wrote down is "publish a book". Why did I not write "publish a bestseller"? And I didn't even mention a holiday home by the beach or a 3-month trip through Canada. I asked for things and experiences that I felt were realistic and achievable. And there's nothing wrong with that but if we want to really open up to anything being possible, we need to step out of our comfort zone.

So today, I want us all to go back to our list and add a few things that fit one of these categories:

1. you think it's impossible
2. you think you don't need it
3. you think you can't have it
4. you don't know how to get it
5. you think you shouldn't want it
6. you think you don't deserve it
7. you think it's embarrassing
8. you feel ashamed or guilty asking for it
9. you feel selfish asking for it
10. you think it's stupid to want it

I'm sure you'll find a few more reasons for not having, wanting or deserving certain things. Why do we even think these thoughts and manipulate ourselves in this way? It's our conditioning. Society, parents, media all tell us what we can and can't have or do and what's appropriate to have and do. And at some point in life, we start believing what they tell us is true and we stop dreaming and believing in what we thought was true.

We're going to work on this today. We're going to start the process of letting go of these limiting beliefs and create new beliefs. "I deserve to have this." "Anything is possible." Here are today's exercises:

Exercise 1: Write down 10 things you're grateful for today.

Exercise 2: Add to your wish list all the things that you felt were too big, unrealistic, ridiculous, selfish, etc.

Exercise 3: Read the complete list with today's and yesterday's wishes. Then add "I deserve to have..." before every item on your list. Read it out loud and do it until you feel comfortable saying it.

And here's another thing I do when I have big dreams and I recommend you to do the same: Surround yourself with other dreamers. I loved watching this video on YouTube: Search for "Stop Telling Your Big Dreams to Small-Minded People".

DAY 4

"The quieter you become, the more you can hear."

—Ram Dass

Good morning magical beings, hope you all had good thoughts when you woke up and feel excited about today. I just had a numerology reading and was reminded about the importance of meditation and being in nature. "The way you start your day is how you live your life" my friend said to me. We're waking up with positive thoughts and writing down 10 things we're grateful for each morning. We should be attracting an amazing life with such an amazing morning practice! And to make it even better, take some time each morning to meditate. When I started, I started with 5 mins, that's all I could do. Then I increased it to 10, then 15 mins. Now I meditate for half an hour. When you have a few minutes of peace and quiet in the morning, where you focus on your breathing and sit still, your day will be a reflection of that. So give it a go today.

Exercise 1: sit in meditation for a few minutes. Close your eyes, take a few deep breaths and just be.

Flavia Waas

Exercise 2: Write down 10 things you're grateful for today.

For the rest of the day, I want us all to daydream! Think of the things you wrote down on your list in the last 2 days. Pick one at a time and visualise them. Visualise living in your amazing home, visualise yourself hiking in Nepal. Feel the cool, thin air as you breathe in. Hear the sound of your feet touching the Earth as you hike up the rocky path. See the clouds moving in the dark blue sky. Feel how it feels to have what you want. You can have a conversation with your future husband, smile at the sight of your future kids playing in the garden, and feel the wind in your hair sailing on your new boat. Immerse yourself into your daydream.

This will do two things:

1. it'll keep you focused on what you want and therefore bring it to you
2. it'll take your focus off the things you don't want.

Exercise 3: daydream! Visualise the things, people and experiences on your list. Feel how it feels to have them. Be grateful for having them, be joyful and happy about having them.

And here's a video I'd recommend you to watch. Doreen Virtue has a story to share about how her family manifested a car by visualising it. Most people think this is ridiculous but as dreamers and master manifesters we know better. This "woo woo stuff" as my friend calls it works!

Search for "Interview with Doreen Virtue" on Youtube.

Have a beautiful day! Enjoy the daydreaming.

DAY
5

It's another beautiful day today, time for some ACTION!

So far we thought about what we want, we wrote it down, we told ourselves that we deserved to have it and we started visualising our dreams. Now it's time for action.

Does that scare you a little bit, taking action? Taking steps towards achieving or having the things you'd like to have? It doesn't have to be overwhelming, the steps can be very small. Remember what Doreen Virtue said in the video I shared yesterday, you take one step at a time.

And: taking action can be fun! Actually, it should always be fun and playful and never feel like a burden or something we have to do. If it does, it may not be time to take action just yet. Maybe we need to overcome fear or let go of other limitations before we're ready. So for now, let's start with what feels easy.

When I started this practice, I used to think too big and too complicated. So I'll give you a few tips and examples to ease your discomfort.

An action can be: researching online, reading a book, talking to an expert, signing up for an online course, going window shopping, creating space for the desired item, person, experience. And like someone suggested to me earlier, creating a vision board on pinterest, thank you! We'll be doing vision boards on the weekend, on pinterest or "old school" with magazines.

I'll give you a few examples of actions and reactions you can take.

You want to go on a holiday? Block out a time in your calendar and write "Fiji trip". When somebody asks to meet you during that time, tell them you won't be available. If you feel confident about going, tell them "I won't be able to meet you, I'll be in Fiji". Get a guidebook about Fiji, research airfares to Fiji, start planning your trip.

You want to attract your soul mate? I once read a book where the author described how she used to sleep in the middle of the bed. When she realised there was no space for anyone other than herself she started sleeping on one side of the bed, making room for her future boyfriend. I also spoke to Andy in my mind before I met him in the flesh. It always felt natural and normal.

You want a new car? Start looking at ads, enquire about prices, visit a car dealer, test drive the car you want. Show genuine interest. The universe will respond.

I bought a self-publishing package 3 years ago when I knew I wanted to write a book. That was my first step and it was challenging because it involved $1,500, which was a lot back then - I had just come home from traveling and had no money. It was my way of saying "universe, I really want this, please show me how to do it." And something magical happened 3 days ago, when I wrote on my list "publish a book." I told Andy that I'll be using the self-publishing package to make "Magical May" into a book. That night, the publishing house called to check how I was going with my book. They call me ONCE a year and they called that night. Can you believe it? Now if that's not magical!

You're acting and you're reacting. Some of these actions and reactions can be a bit out of your comfort zone but since we're taking small steps, we can handle the discomfort.

Exercise 1: sit in meditation for a few minutes. Close your eyes, take a few deep breaths and just be.

Exercise 2: Write down 10 things you're grateful for today.

Exercise 3: Take action. Take small steps towards your dreams. Don't force it, do things that are fun and don't feel too uncomfortable to begin with.

And you're welcome to daydream again too. That's something we should never stop doing. The more time we spend on thinking about what we want, the less time we spend on thinking about what we don't want and therefore we attract what we want, it's that simple.

There's an inspiring video about "How to Move" on YouTube. Check it out!

DAY
6

"You know the truth by the way it feels."

—Unknown

Good morning day 6! Yesterday was all about action, taking steps towards your dreams and goals. Which may be easy for some of the items on your list and a bit harder for others. If you have no clue what the first step is, today's for you.

If I don't know what to do, I ask the universe. "What do I need to do to get xyz?" Then I wait for an answer. But how does the universe respond? Is it a voice telling you, "call this person" or "go to this place"? Maybe that's what the universe replies with but can you hear it?

I remember when I first heard "the voice". It was on a flight from Australia to Germany. I was moving back to Germany and was very excited to be with my old friends and family again. When suddenly a voice said "you won't stay here for long." I looked around to see where the voice came from but nobody was there. It was the voice in my head.

But I don't hear that voice all the time and I don't get clear messages like that every time I ask. So luckily, there's another way to receive messages from "above". And that's in the form of signs and clues. And I give you an example for signs and clues as well.

Shortly after "the voice" spoke to me on the plane I arrived in Munich and was welcomed by my family and a few close friends. One of them looked at me and said "I give you one year, two years max." What? Was it so obvious to everyone that I wasn't going to stay here?

And a friend of my mum made a similar comment. And even though I ignored the signs at first, I never forgot what these people said. A few months later it all made sense and I saw it myself and moved back to Australia.

And I got another beautiful sign to go back to Australia when I lived in Hawaii. I wanted to stay and tried to figure out how to do it. But the universe had other plans for me. One day I sat down in a cafe. My coffee arrived and on the creamy top bit the brown of the coffee had painted the perfect outlines of the Australian continent. Including Tasmania hanging at the bottom. I stared at the coffee, I couldn't believe what I saw. Shortly after that, more signs were put in front of me and I knew I was going back to Australia.

Signs can come as written words, in a book, magazine, a street sign, license plate or shop window. Signs can pop up in a conversation, a friend calling you, a stranger talking to you or just you overhearing a conversation. It can be words in a song on the radio or on the news.

Signs can be smells that remind you of a place. I often get signs through pictures, photographs, and paintings. Signs can also come as injury. You may see a specific healer or doctor with that injury who gives you an important clue. And when you look back at the chain of events later, it suddenly all makes sense. Signs can just be a beautiful rainbow that makes you think "yes, I'm in the right place."

Signs can also come through animals. I've always been drawn to the Native American culture and the idea of animal totems. Numbers can give you clues as well. Numerology is something else I'm fascinated by. You can add to this list, I'm sure there are signs everywhere.

What's important in order for you to see the signs and recognise them as such, is to be open and observe your environment. Become a good observer and a good listener. Get out of your mind and create space to receive new information and messages.

Today's exercises:

Exercise 1: sit in meditation for a few minutes. Close your eyes, take a few deep breaths and just be.

Exercise 2: Write down 10 things you're grateful for today.

Exercise 3: Observe what's happening around you. Listen intently when somebody speaks, keep your eyes open, BE PRESENT.

Go to YouTube for are a few more helpful tips on "How to receive signs from the universe"

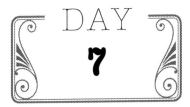

DAY 7

"To the mind that is still the whole universe surrenders."

—Lao Tzu

How are we all feeling on this beautiful Saturday morning? Do you need a break? Great, because we're having a break today. We won't be thinking, visualising, writing, taking steps towards our goals or watching out for signs. We'll just relax and practice the art of LETTING GO.

While it's important to focus on what we want rather than what we don't want, we have to be careful not to become obsessed with what we want. It's ok to follow the signs and visualise but this needs to happen from a place of love, not fear.

When you think about what you want from a place of love, you feel relaxed, happy, content, confident, joyful, and excited. You know it's going to happen. No, you know it's already happened. You're grateful for having this thing on your list because it feels like it's already there. This is where we want to be.

When you come from a place of fear, you feel impatient, frustrated, and anxious. You feel a lack of this thing on your list. You wonder if it's really going to happen and when. You're hoping it will come but you have trouble believing it, let alone knowing it. You become obsessed thinking about it. This is what we want to avoid.

So today, let's just forget about our list for a while and relax. Just let it go, don't think about it, be in the moment. And watch how hard or easy this is for you. Have you become obsessed with wanting something and not having it? Or do you already feel like you have it? It's not in your physical experience yet but it's there, you've manifested it, you can feel it, you can just let it go.

A good way to let go is to simply focus on something else. In our case, we'll be focusing on something that makes us feel good. Because feeling good will attract more of - feeling good. What makes your heart sing? A walk in nature? A yummy breakfast? A bike ride, chat with a good friend, reading a book, sitting on the beach, walking your dog, playing with your child, going to the movies, eating pizza?

Do exactly that today and enjoy every single moment. Be present, be in the flow, and celebrate life.

Exercise 1: sit in meditation for a few minutes. Close your eyes, take a few deep breaths and just be.

Exercise 2: Write down 10 things you're grateful for today.

Exercise 3: Do whatever makes you feel happy.

DAY
8

Good morning to another beautiful day with endless possibilities. Today we're going to talk about TIME and how it plays a role in manifesting.

What we need to be aware of is that things come to us when the time is right, in "divine timing" as we call it. And that can lead to frustration when we have our own ideas about timing. To be more precise, when our ego has its own ideas about timing.

When we wrote our list with the things we wanted I asked you to think about the "why". Why do you want something? How does it make you feel? And we need to ask the same question about the timing we're expecting things to arrive in our physical reality.

Why do we want our soul mate to come into our lives by the end of June? There's probably no real reason other than "because I've been waiting for so long and I'm getting impatient." Often we put a deadline in place because we're loosing hope. We don't trust that we'll really get what we want. We want proof!

But it can also work out and we do get things at the time we asked for them to arrive. I once needed a new car because my car had broken down and I asked for it to be delivered within 4 days. And I got it in 4 days because I needed it. I had no car, so there was room for a new car.

As we know, the law of attraction always brings to us what we focus on and will always match our vibration. So impatience will bring more impatience. And by the end of June we're upset because the soul mate hasn't appeared and we have proof that manifesting doesn't work because we didn't get what we wanted. When really, we did get what we asked for - more impatience.

The main reason why it worked for me was that I wasn't impatient and I didn't doubt that the car would come. I just knew it. And I wasn't attached to getting it within 4 days either. If it had taken twice as long, fine. I was already making plans to riding the bike into town. That could have been fun, great for fitness too. I was detached from the outcome.

We practiced letting go yesterday and this is a very important one when it comes to manifesting. Ask for it, feel it, believe it, visualise it and then let it go. Don't get stuck on time, because it'll backfire at you. The more impatient you are, the more reason for impatience you'll get.

A psychic once told me "time is helping you" and I didn't get what he meant at first. Later it made sense. I needed time to get ready for certain things. I couldn't have met my husband 5 years ago, I wasn't ready. I needed to learn a few lessons, open up, and let go.

So always see time as your friend. Time prepares you, time helps you to be ready to receive the things on your list and not push them away when they come along. Time helps you to get over your fear of the thing, person, and experience being too big to handle.

Have you ever felt anxious because you set yourself a deadline? That's another example of being stuck on time. It can help to work with a deadline if you're working towards something – like writing a book for example – but if it becomes stressful and you feel under pressure, you need to remove this deadline. It feels so good when you do. Suddenly you feel like you have all the time in the world. So remove any deadlines from your wish list and see how that makes you feel. Don't pressure the universe, the universe doesn't need deadlines. It operates in divine timing!

Exercise 1: sit in meditation for a few minutes. Close your eyes, take a few deep breaths and just be.

Exercise 2: Write down 10 things you're grateful for today.

Exercise 3: Look at the deadlines you've placed on certain events, things or people and ask yourself why you've set a date. Was it out of a real need (like needing food so you don't starve) or out of impatience and a lack of trust that it's really going to happen?

DAY
9

"Nobody can make you feel inferior without your consent."

—Eleanor Roosevelt

Is there an area in your life where everything just works out? Where things are flowing effortlessly? Have you always been healthy, had a good job, great relationships, enough money? For me it's been my work. After a few difficulties – it took me quite some time to find a job when I finished uni – I found my dream job. And it's been a smooth ride ever since. I would go to interviews with an "I don't care" attitude and always get the job. I always knew what I wanted and didn't settle for less. I always knew my worth. I always trusted that there'll be another job for me. I never felt there was a lack of jobs, I never believed in competition. I even considered quitting in case I wouldn't be allowed the amount of time off I wanted. Before talking to my boss I would say to myself "If he/she says no, I'll quit." And I was dead serious. And I always got my holiday approved.

When I started to look at myself and my patterns I noticed that and I wondered, how can I apply what I do in my job to the rest of my life? And what were the "secret" ingredients for the success I was having? I've identified the following ones:

1. Be confident

Know what you're good at, know your worth. Not just as an employee like in this example, know your worth as a human being. If somebody criticizes you, how do you take it? Do you think "he's right, I'm not that great." Or do you think "that's just his opinion, I know I'm great." If you have self-confidence, nobody will question you and nobody will deny you anything. If you not just accept yourself but love yourself, everybody else will too. Whether it's a partner or a boss or co-worker.

2. Trust

I talked about coming from a place of love versus a place of fear before. You could also say, coming from a place of trust versus a place of doubt. Every time I asked my boss about taking time off, I did so from a place of trust. I know people who don't even want to ask for time off, let alone a lot of time off because they fear they'll loose their job. They place so much value on this particular job, they start valuing it more than themselves. They don't trust that there's another job out there for them, a better job. That's not a good position for any negotiation. Instead, be detached from the outcome and trust in the process. Know that whatever happens, you'll be fine. If you trust, you'll be able to speak up, ask for what you want and voice your opinion clearly. Very important not just in a job but in any relationship with a romantic partner, family or friends.

3. Know what you want

When you know what you want, it's much easier for the universe to respond – we all know that by now. It's also much easier for your boss to respond when you're clear about what you want. To stay with the example, asking for leave, know when you want to go and how long for. There's no "whenever it's convenient for you" or "if it's ok" or "if it's not too much to ask". If it's not convenient for them, they'll tell you. So know what you want and ask for it. And if you know that you'll quit otherwise, great. I assume that if it came to you telling your boss you'll quit he would try everything to make your holiday possible and keep you. And if not, that's great too. At least you know how little you're appreciated and have an opportunity to create a better situation for yourself. This also applies to any type of relationships. Don't let the other walk all over you, know what you want and communicate it clearly.

Exercise 1: sit in meditation for a few minutes. Close your eyes, take a few deep breaths and just be.

Exercise 2: Write down 10 things you're grateful for today.

Exercise 3: look at your life and identify an area where things have always worked out. What are the success factors? Is it confidence, trust and clarity? Are there any other beliefs you have that seem to make it work for you? Ask yourself, "how can I apply this to other areas in my life?"

DAY
10

"Logic will get you from A to B. Imagination will take you everywhere."

—Albert Einstein

Good morning magic makers. By now, writing down 10 things you're grateful for, feels easy. Would you agree? It's become part of my routine, just like brushing my teeth. And so will all the other exercises, as you repeat them over and over again.

I promised you a vision board for the weekend and I totally forgot, oops. The universe must have had other plans and that's exactly what I was talking about two days ago: divine timing, not your ego's timing. So we're doing the vision board today and because some of you may be working full time, you'll have the whole week to complete it.

I wrote an article about vision boards a few months ago so just follow the instructions below:

Ever since I got introduced to vision boards a few years ago, I've been cutting and glueing my dreams into reality by making vision boards. A powerful and fun way to manifest the life you want. If you've never made a vision board before, this is how it's done.

First of all, you need a vision. If you have no idea what you want to create in your life, what do you stick onto your vision board? Think about what you'd like to manifest for yourself - a home, a boyfriend/girlfriend, time in nature, a gucci handbag, publishing a book, making lots of money, a horse, travel, studying art, playing in a punk rock band, losing 20 pounds, making your own jewellery, a lap pool - whatever it might be. And go nuts, don't be modest, pretend that there are no limits. I always ask people "what would you do if money wasn't an issue?" Don't think about money or time or whether you or other people think it's realistic. Just allow yourself to have it all on your vision board.

Then you need magazines. I usually buy magazines as "dreaming aids" - I love interior design, travel, health, fashion and lifestyle magazines and find most of the images I need for my vision board in the magazines I already have. I have bought "men's health" on one occasion because I needed a nice picture of a man to stick on my vision board, ideally Hugh Jackman, who was luckily featured in "men's health" that month. I also bought a girl's surf magazine because I needed a picture of a female surfer inside a barrel. You can make vision boards online and simply copy and paste images you find online but I like the idea of physically cutting and pasting and for once, not staring at a screen.

You'll find that as you're going through your stack of magazines, your vision might change. You wanted an outdoor shower? How about an outdoor bath tub as well, on a private deck overlooking the jungle. I often find stuff in magazines that I didn't even know existed and that's so good, I couldn't have made it up myself. You might be a bit shy at first, trying to decide whether you want the house on the beach or the cabin in the mountains. Why not stick both of them onto your vision board. You need a holiday retreat, right? And why not get the 4WD and the convertible, there are no limits. You can be a bestselling author, devoted mother, extreme skier and 5 star chef all at the same time.

Once you've stuck everything onto your board, put it up somewhere where you can see it. Add to it if you find more good stuff in magazines or take things off when you've changed your mind. We've still got a few empty spaces on our vision board. My partner and I made one together a while ago, to manifest a place to live. It's full of beautiful pictures of farm land, forest, waterfalls, farm houses, vegetables, flowers, a donkey and yes, an outdoor shower AND outdoor bath, no compromises.

The last very important step is to trust that it's coming to you in divine timing. Don't push it, don't try to make it happen, don't get upset or impatient when it's taking a bit longer. The universe always delivers.

Are you inspired? The article explained how to do the "old school" vision boards, with cardboard, scissors, glue and a few magazines. But you can also sign up to pinterest and create a virtual vision board by browsing the Internet for pictures you like and then pinning them onto your pinterest board. I've done a few old school ones and gave pinterest a go this time.

I'd also like to share a recent manifestation success story. Andy and I talked about mountains and I told him about the Alps. We got a map out and I showed him how they span across Italy, France, Switzerland, Germany and Austria. I told him about some of my ski trips and I also told him how amazing it is to fly across the Alps. To be so close to the sharp, snow capped peaks, especially on a clear and sunny day.

In the evening after dinner I took my phone and went on Facebook. I didn't really know why, it's nothing I usually do. But as I was opening Facebook, the first picture I saw was a picture of the Alps, taken from a plane. My friend was on her way back from Italy to Germany and had posted a few beautiful pictures, just like I had described it to Andy - clear blue skies with the sharp white peaks of the mountains. I showed it to him and said "I don't know if you manifested this or I did, but here's a picture of what I described to you earlier".

It made us both happy and to me, these synchronicities are not just coincidences, they're pure magic. And it's not magic happening to us, we create it.

So if you ever get stuck on the big things on your list taking so long to manifest - watch out for the little things. Things that seem to be unimportant. And when you realise you've manifested something small like this, be grateful for it and excited to have proof that you are a powerful manifestor.

Exercise 1: sit in meditation for a few minutes. Close your eyes, take a few deep breaths and just be.

Exercise 2: Write down 10 things you're grateful for today.

Exercise 3: Create a vision board, "old school" or on pinterest.

DAY
11

"Let food be thy medicine and medicine be thy food."

—Hippocrates

I hope you had fun with the vision board yesterday! Keep your eyes open for inspiring pictures to cut out and if you've done it on pinterest, keep your eyes open while you're on your computer.

Today and the following 4 days we'll be diving deeper into different areas of our lives and observe our beliefs. We'll be looking at health, finances, home, relationships and work and ask ourselves, "am I in alignment with my dreams and desires?".

If you've been listening to Abraham Hicks for a bit, you will have noticed that he talks a lot about being in the vortex and raising your vibration to match the vibration of your desires. And that's what we're going to do.

The first area we'll be looking at is our health. A lot of us have something like 'perfect health' on our wish lists. And just like with everything else that we've asked for, we will be guided to take steps towards a healthier life. So watch for the signs!

One big factor of perfect health is nutrition. "You are what you eat." I don't know who said it but I live by it. I also like the saying "my body is my temple." So look at your food choices today. Do you feed your body nutritious, organic, clean whole foods? Or processed food that's full of artificial colouring, artificial flavours, stabilisers, preservatives and GMOs? Science has now proved that cancer is a man made disease that didn't occur before we started living in the toxic, polluted environment we're living in now. So make sure you choose what you put into your body wisely, you don't want to make yourself sick. Look at the ingredients list when you buy something. You'll find that a lot of seemingly healthy foods are full of preservatives. Try to buy local and organic. Or even better, grow your own!

I'd recommend for you to also observe how you eat. It's important to enjoy the food we're eating and not feel guilty or bad about eating something. If you think this piece of chocolate is bad for you, it will be. Remember? The law of attraction? Your thoughts create your experiences. So stop labeling food that you love "bad". If you feel like you're eating a lot of bad foods and you just can't stop it, look at why you're doing it. Why are you manipulating yourself in this way? Why are you overeating or under eating? Is it to fill an emotional hole? It maybe a good idea to find some books about the psychology behind food addictions.

Another big factor is movement of your body. I recently read a book where they let 70 and 80 year olds go back to the gym. Their theory was, "if you don't use it, you lose it." So they wanted to see what happens when you get back into exercising. Not only did their flexibility and strength improve, their biological age changed. While the chronological age (measured from birth) always stays the same, the biological age can improve. Exercise will keep you young and fit and is so good for your mind as well. You release endorphins, which reduce depression and boost happiness. They're also called the 'happy hormones'. If exercising is hard for you, remember that walking is exercise too. So is riding the bike. And I'm not talking about bike racing, just getting from A to B on a bike at a normal speed.

Last but not least, sleep. We laugh when we say I need my "beauty sleep". But it's true, sleep does keep you beautiful. So many of us get sick because they're sleep deprived. It's recommended to sleep between 7 and 8 hours, so give yourself the sleep you need. That too will keep you healthy, young and beautiful.

I'm sure there's more to health but these are my personal winners and I'm constantly trying to improve my health and find the right balance for me.

Exercise 1: sit in meditation for a few minutes. Close your eyes, take a few deep breaths and just be.

Exercise 2: Write down 10 things you're grateful for today.

Exercise 3: Look at your eating, exercise and sleeping habits and make steps towards improving your health.

DAY 12

"You are the average of the five people you spend the most time with."

—Jim Rohn

Good morning creators, another beautiful day and a new opportunity to make it an amazing day. We're not moving on to the next area of our lives just yet, we'll be looking at our HEALTH again today because I'd like to add a few very important bits here.

Yesterday we looked at the foods we put into our bodies, today we'll be looking at the information we put into our bodies. We now know that our thoughts and the words we use when we speak or write create our reality. But not just our own words, any words, written or spoken, that we expose ourselves to every day.

In your mind, go through your day and look at what kind of information you take in. You may listen to the radio, talk to your partner, kids, friends, colleagues. You read the paper or a magazine, watch the news, a movie or documentary. Are your conversations positive? Are the programs you watch helping your manifestation process in any way? Or are they hindering it? I never thought about my information intake contributing to my wellbeing until I studied "Holistic Counseling". Since we were taking a holistic approach to life, we weren't just looking at our minds, we were looking at every area of our lives, including the environment we live in, the people we deal with and the information we consume.

And I'll give you a few examples so you can look at your patterns when it comes to information intake.

First of all, let's look at the interaction with other people. Do the people you surround yourself with have a positive attitude towards life? Or do they have beliefs like "life is hard"? Are they constantly broke, sick and complaining how bad they've got it?

If so, you may want to reconsider hanging out with them. We often feel like we need to help people like this, cheer them up, and make them feel better. But the truth is, only they can make themselves feel better. And how are you feeling after you've had an hour of negativity? Are you still joyful? Are you still vibrating on the same frequency as your desires and dreams? Probably not. So make sure to spend time with people who have a positive energy. Remember what Oprah said in the interview I shared the other day, "Surround yourself with fellow dreamers."

It's also important to make the right choices when it comes to watching TV, listening to the radio and reading books, magazines and newspapers.

Let's talk about the news. Do you feel the news are a reflection of what's really going on in the world or do we only get the filtered version, the information that "they" want us to have. Are the news positive and full of good advice that helps us to live a better life? Or are they fear creating, keeping us small and obedient?

Don't feel obliged to watch or read the news to stay "informed". What kind of information are we getting that's really important for us? The news are just one opinion, showing one side of the story. It's a good idea to find alternative sources to stay informed.

And I want to touch on movies and TV series as well. Are you watching comedies or dramas or even horror movies? Why? Is that what you want to attract into your life? Wouldn't you rather watch something uplifting, funny, intelligent, charming, and beautiful?

Andy and I started watching a very popular TV series last year. But every episode was so brutal and cruel, we stopped watching it. There was one particular episode that made me so upset, I needed some time to get back to my normal self. After that incidence, we deleted the whole season from our computer and never watched it again. It wasn't at all in alignment with what I wanted in my life.

Exercise 1: sit in meditation for a few minutes. Close your eyes, take a few deep breaths and just be.

Exercise 2: Write down 10 things you're grateful for today.

Exercise 3: Look at your information intake. Who do you hang out with? What do you read and watch? Make a change!

On YouTube you'll find a few good tips from Marie Forleo. One is about how to break up with a negative friend. Search for "Positive People" And the other one about "Are people around you holding you back?"

DAY
13

"If I ever go looking for my heart's desire again, I won't look any further than my own back yard. Because if it isn't there, I never really lost it to begin with."

—L. Frank Baum, The Wonderful Wizard of Oz

How did you go with yesterday's exercise? It can be heartbreaking to see how some of our closest friends and family members are draining us. And realising that their negativity can throw us off our path can be confronting. Most of us wouldn't want to just "break up" with them. So find ways to change the conversation or, if you feel they're open to it, talk to them and make them aware of what they're doing to you and most importantly to themselves by being negative, feeling sorry for themselves and complaining all the time.

We're moving on to the next area today, our HOME. The basic needs of human beings are food, shelter and love. We're lucky, most of us are living in places where there's an abundance of food, and shelter is provided for everyone. Depending on the social system of your country you won't have to worry about a home, you're taken care of and can live comfortably, even when you don't have an income to pay for housing. And most of us have more than just a shelter, we live in beautiful houses. They may not be our dream home but that's what we're working on manifesting. How many of you have "my dream home" on your list? I certainly do and I also have a holiday house on my list and the wish to live comfortably wherever I go. Whether it's a hotel or a friend's place, I like to feel home everywhere.

The key to attracting your dream home is to visualise it and feel it like it's already there. It's easy to imagine being there and really feeling it when you're already living in an amazing house. It's not so easy to feel it when your current living situation sucks. So again, we need to focus on the positive side of things and say thanks for what we have.

Maybe your place is too small but it's in a great location: "I'm so grateful to be living in such an amazing location." Your place may be spacious but freezing cold in winter. Focus on the spaciousness, not the cold. I for myself have decided not to be cold this winter. I don't know how often I used the word "cold" last winter and I'm so over it. I'll be focusing on winter being cozy and warm and comfortable. Because that's how I'd like winter to be in my dream home.

You can also take steps towards your new home by looking at houses for rent or sale or, if you want to build a house, draw plans. I can't tell you how much fun it was to draw plans for our house. And I started way before we had found the land to build it on. Pinterest is a great way to look at houses or simply Google houses. I looked at infinity pools on Google the other day, so much fun.

I also have a wish list in my IKEA account where I keep adding things that I want to have. And I know I'll have them because in my mind, I've already furnished the whole house with them.

And watch your thoughts while going through this process. Do you think "oh, I wish, but it's too expensive" or do you think "it's perfect, I love it and I can manifest the money easily." And maybe you don't even have to buy it, maybe it's given to you. Andy always says "don't say "buy", say "get". Or even better, "receive"." We don't want to close ourselves to the possibility of receiving stuff for free.

Another secret to manifesting a home is to feel home inside. To feel grounded and solid and safe and all the other feelings that you expect a home to give you. Feel it now as if it's already there. The reason why I live in beautiful homes everywhere I go is because I feel home everywhere I go - the benefits of having a gypsy soul.

And last but not least, let it go. Don't obsess about it, don't put a deadline on it, and don't get impatient. It'll come, it has to. It's the law!

Exercise 1: sit in meditation for a few minutes. Close your eyes, take a few deep breaths and just be.

Exercise 2: Write down 10 things you're grateful for today.

Exercise 3: Watch your thoughts about your current living situation. Find things to be grateful for about your home now. Actively look for the things you like in a home. Go window-shopping at the real estate agencies for example!

DAY
14

"How do you spell 'love'?" – Piglet "You don't spell it...you feel it." - Pooh"

—A.A. Milne, Winnie the Pooh

Good morning everyone, today's the day we're talking about relationships. Not just love relationships, any relationships - with your friends, your co-workers, your family an your partner. But also with strangers - a waitress in a cafe, a call center employee, the postman. We want any interaction with another human being to be pleasant.

I don't want to bore you but the same principle applies here. First of all, have gratitude for the people that are in your life right now. Focus on the positive characteristics of a person rather than the negative.

If you want to change the dynamics of a relationship with someone who's already in your life, you may want to change your attitude towards them. I read somewhere that if you want to dance a different dance, somebody needs to make a start and change the steps or the rhythm. The only person you can control is you. So start dancing a different dance and see how the other person reacts. If he or she is willing to dance a new dance, your relationship can change for the better. If not, at least you've tried and someone more suitable will come along. You may also just limit the time spent with someone, give yourself a break from each other. If you don't know what to say, needing "me time" is always a good one.

If you want to attract new people into your life, just ask the universe, put your order in. I remember asking the universe for a spiritual friend. That was when I first started reading about the law of attraction and realising that there's something else to life than the world we can see and touch. And I did meet this person, not long after I asked for her. I also told you that I had conversations with Andy before I met him. Talk to your soul mate, twin flame, life partner. And imagine how life together will be and really feel it. You can do the same with friends. If you're missing a true friend, who's loyal and caring and fun, who can relate to you and who gives you space and doesn't judge you, imagine how life would be if you had that friend.

And very important, don't get into the "poor me" energy where you feel like "nobody loves me" and you feel you're alone. That won't bring you the desired relationships. Do the opposite, tell yourself that everybody loves you and wants to hang out with you. Have you noticed how happy children are who have an "imaginary friend"? They play together, talk together, and laugh together. They're having the best time "alone". Because they know that the unseen is just as real as the seen. So make lots of new imaginary friends. They will soon become a physical reality.

And spend time with people who love you and accept you and treat you with respect. Spend time with the people you can have fun with and go on adventures. Avoid negative, draining people and conversations altogether. I've done it before, leaving a cafe early because I couldn't take it anymore. "Sorry guys, I gotta make a move." No explanation needed, you have "stuff to do" if somebody wants to know.

Also, be aware of how you treat yourself and how you communicate with yourself. I wrote an article once about giving yourself the things that you'd like others to give you. I used flowers as an example. If they make you happy, get some. Don't wait for someone to buy them for you. Your husband may not even know that you like flowers because he never sees any around the house.

And practice positive self-talk. Don't say "I'm so stupid" or "I'm useless". Others can only treat you as good as you treat yourself so don't underestimate the importance of the relationship you have with yourself.

Last but not least, make sure your actions are aligned with your desires. A lot of people say they want to be loved by their partner for their whole being - body, mind and soul. And what do they do? They get involved with someone who wants to have a "casual" relationship or they have a proper relationship but with someone they don't really love. While in these relationships, they hope someone better will come along. But what's the message they put out to the universe? It's "casual is perfectly fine for me" or "I'm happy to be with anyone". Your actions speak louder than words so don't think one thing and then do something completely opposite.

Exercise 1: sit in meditation for a few minutes. Close your eyes, take a few deep breaths and just be.

Exercise 2: Write down 10 things you're grateful for today.

Exercise 3: Be grateful for the good relationships you have. Talk to the people you'd like to attract into your lives – "real" people or "imagined" people. Improve the relationship you have with yourself. That'll automatically improve all your relationships.

DAY
15

"Sometimes good things fall apart so better things can fall together."

—Marilyn Monroe

Happy weekend! We'll be talking about WORK today. Yes, on a Saturday. If you've made your passion your profession you probably don't mind thinking about work on a weekend. If that's not the case and you feel stuck in an unfulfilling job, here's how you can change it.

Again we'll be starting by finding things about our current work that we're grateful for. I didn't enjoy my last job at the end but what I did enjoy every time was the way to work. I was always grateful for the ferry ride in the morning and the beautiful location our office was in. And there were some very nice people working with me as well so there were a lot of positive aspects to it. Try to find things you like about your current job.

You've probably all got work on your list. Ideally, most of us want to feel fulfilled, appreciated, enjoy their work, don't work too hard, get paid well and do something they love. And you can have it all but it may require some big changes.

There are 3 options to finding the work you love - actually, these 3 options are available for any situation. If you're unhappy with a (work) situation you can a) accept it b) change it or c) remove yourself from it. It's that simple.

If you can't accept the situation, we can cross out option a). But maybe you can improve your situation. You can visualise a better situation, you can visualise your boss giving you a pay rise or promoting you or whatever it is you'd like to have. And then there will be a time where you'll need to act. You need to say "yes" or "no" to certain questions and if nobody offers you the things you want, you need to be brave, speak up and ask for it!

And if that doesn't do anything either, you need to consider option c) and that's what most people struggle with the most. Because you have to take a leap of faith. Sometimes you'll just have to quit a job or invest into a project without knowing what comes next.

And these are the situations when you need to listen to your gut feeling and watch the signs. My last job is a good example. I wanted to leave and decided I'd quit. Just making that decision in my mind felt so good! So I knew it would happen.

I knew I wanted to do my own thing but only had one potential client to begin with. Then a headhunter called me and offered me a high paying job at another agency. I saw it as a sign and went to meet her. We had a conversation after the interview and I told her I was thinking of doing my own thing. She said "you need to do it. Your whole face lit up when you started talking about it." And that's how I knew. And sure enough, as soon as word got out that I had left my job, the offers came. In a very short period of time I had more than enough clients to make a living.

In other situations we're forced to leave. We get made redundant, we get bullied or we suffer a nervous breakdown - we're literally "sick of work". Could the signs be any clearer? It's time for you to move on!

When we write on our list "I want to be more valued and appreciated in my job" we may expect an improvement in our current job. But don't be surprised when it doesn't happen and instead we are asked to leave. It just means what we've asked for isn't possible in our current job, only a new job will lead us there.

So don't see endings as something bad. They sometimes need to happen so we can have a better experience. I have a good affirmation for this one. "I'm always in the right place, at the right time, doing the right thing." I think I borrowed this quote from Louise Hay. And if something unexpected and unwanted happens, I tell myself "it must be good because I'm always in the right place, at the right time, doing the right thing. This "bad thing" that's happening to me now must be for the greater good, because I only manifest amazing things."

Know that if you ask for something amazing and your current situation is not so amazing, big changes will need to happen. They may feel scary or uncomfortable at first but all new things do. Susan Jeffers, author of "Feel the fear and do it anyway" says the fear will never go away. It'll always creep in when you do something you've never done before. Don't let that fear rule your life.

Exercise 1: sit in meditation for a few minutes. Close your eyes, take a few deep breaths and just be.

Exercise 2: Write down 10 things you're grateful for today.

Exercise 3: Find things to be grateful for in your current work situation. Watch the signs, trust your gut feeling, take action when it feels good (even if it's a little bit scary, it'll be for the better.)

DAY 16

"If you change the way you look at things, the things you look at change."

—Wayne Dyer

Good morning my magical friends! We've talked about health, home, relationships and work, we haven't talked about MONEY yet. How's your financial situation? Have you "made it" or are you struggling? Wouldn't it be nice if money was something we didn't even have to talk about because it's just there, naturally, all the time?

We place an immense value on money. We rely on money to give us a sense of security. Our happiness depends on money. Having little money makes us feel sad, unworthy, insecure, fearful. And if we have it, we want to hold on to it, because it makes us feel safe. And from that fear of not feeling safe, we just spend it, on stuff we don't need. And we're back where we started, we don't have any money and we feel uncomfortable. Isn't that insane?

Just like people have eating disorders they have money disorders too. You're not allowed to eat it so you want to eat it more and when you do, you feel bad about it. This is how a lot of people spend money. They don't allow themselves to spend it on, say clothes, so they want to spend it even more and when they do they don't feel any better, they actually feel worse. Terrible.

How can we attract a better financial situation into our lives if this is our pattern? It would be very difficult, so let's change it and think and feel abundantly.

Step 1 is as usual, to be grateful for they money you have right now. Are you living in a house, eating food every day? How lucky are you. And if you've been watching some of the YouTube videos I recommended, you've also got access to a computer or phone with WIFI. Most likely, money bought all this. So you're not poor, you don't lack anything. That's a good starting point. Don't you think?

After you've given gratitude for the money you have, think about all the things you'd like to buy for the money you're asking for. Because when you ask for a million dollars you don't really want the money, you want the things this money can buy, right? So visualise yourself buying a new car or your dream home. And remember, you may not have to buy it, you may just "get" it or "receive" it from somebody else. So leave it up to the universe how you receive your car or home.

And here's a very important one: You need to believe that there's enough money. Someone else having more money doesn't mean you'll have less money. Everyone including yourself can have a piece of the cake. Maybe we can all have a whole cake!

Also, money is energy and energy needs to move. Don't sit on your money, spend it. Make room for more money. I'll empty my bank account tomorrow to buy my dream car and I feel great about it because I know, more money will come. Look back at your life so far, hasn't money always come back in? So trust that it'll continue to be like that. Spend those $250 on a night in a luxurious hotel. You won't miss that money 5 years down the track but you'll still talk about this amazing experience in 5 years time.

I saw a book cover once and it said "the secret of having money, is having money". And without reading the book, I got it. When we have money, we feel rich and abundant so we attract more of it. So put yourself into a place where you feel rich and abundant right now so you can create more of it. One way of doing this is to always have cash in your wallet. Of course you feel broke when you open your wallet and there's just a few coins in it. I started carrying at least $100 with me and, especially in the beginning, I was surprised each time I opened my wallet. "Oh, I didn't know I had that much money!" were my thoughts each time I saw the dollar bills. It seems silly but it works. You'll start repeating to yourself "wow I've got so much money" several times per day, every time you open our wallet. Your thoughts create your reality. Thinking you have a lot of money will bring a lot of money to you.

I also have a few $100 bills lying around at home, where I can see them. In Feng Shui there's the theory of a "prosperity corner". Find that corner and place some money there. You'll feel rich with all this money lying around the house, trust me.

Another "trick" is to never say "I can't buy this" or "I can't afford this." Say "I choose not to buy this right now". Because the truth is, you are able to afford it. "I can't afford a new car." Well, maybe not right now but if you put $1,000 aside each month, you will be very soon. So don't be a victim who "can't". Be in control and "choose".

And I love this one, I read it in a book, most likely "Money and the law of attraction". With the $100 you carry around with you, go window-shopping. In your imagination, spend those $100 as often as you like on something you see. You're not actually buying it but you could, if you chose to.

Another action you can take is to actually go out and spend it. Treat yourself to something nice. A massage or a new pair of boots. And when you thought you've spent enough, sit down, have a coffee and a big piece of cake. On the way home, stop at the florist and buy yourself a big bunch of flowers. Doesn't that feel good? If you feel guilty, get into the habit of putting money aside for the purpose of having fun. I call it "fun money". The rule is, you're not allowed to feel guilty when spending the fun money. You have to enjoy it and feel good about it.

All the money we have, we'll spend eventually. Whether it's on food or holidays or taxes or massages, it doesn't matter. So we may as well feel good about spending it. The secret is to spend it all and still feel abundant. To not let money rule your life and be responsible for your mood swings. It's just money, it's energy and it can be manifested in large quantities, just like everything else.

Exercise 1: sit in meditation for a few minutes. Close your eyes, take a few deep breaths and just be.

Exercise 2: Write down 10 things you're grateful for today.

There's a great video on YouTube, search for "Arnold Patent – Money".

DAY
17

"It's impossible" said pride. "It's risky" said experience. "It's pointless" said reason. "Give it a try" whispered the heart."

—Unknown

Good morning everyone, hope you had time to finish your vision board last week? If not, don't worry. It'll probably never be finished because once you've attracted everything that you've asked for, you'll have new dreams and desires. So your vision board will grow. Or you can just make another one, that's how I usually do it.

We've talked a lot about visualising the things that we want and feeling how it feels to have them in our lives. This is something you'll never stop doing. You'll "play pretend" until you believe it. And that's what some people don't realize. It's simple but not necessarily easy. Until you truly believe you can have everything you want, until you become a master of manifestation, you need to practice and study and repeat all that you've learned over and over again.

But how do we receive the things that we want into our lives? It may be very simple in some cases. You've asked for a new place to live, you looked through the ads in the paper, you found it, and you got it. Done!

Other times it's not so straightforward. I myself asked for a place at the end of 2014. The place I was living in had been sold and the new owner wanted to move in. I started browsing ads on gumtree and all I could find were overpriced holes. I feared that if I focused one more second on these ugly places that were for rent, I'd create exactly that experience for myself. So I did something else instead, I put this message out to the universe, via Facebook:

"Dear Universe, and Facebook friends and friends of friends, this is what I want for Christmas, or ideally a week before: A beautiful home near Tallows with lovely housemate(s), a wrap around veranda, day beds, hot outdoor shower and a lush green garden. Ideally with fruit trees - Mango and Tahitian lime, yum - an avocado tree, a frangipani tree, hibiscus and gardenias. And a herb garden. A kitchen with a skylight would be great too, I just love skylights! If anyone has a place like that and is looking for an AMAZING housemate, please do let me know. In the meantime I'll be reading "Seaside Interiors" and my "real living" magazines and pour all my energy into manifesting and feeling my dream home coming to me. Ah, feels better already....."

A few seconds later a friend of mine posted an ad, they were looking for a housemate. Even though they didn't have the fruit trees, day bed, hot outdoor shower and wrap around verandah, it felt good, so I went to see the place. You may think, "but this isn't what you've asked for!" And it wasn't but it had so many other good aspects, like lovely housemates, a huge room, my own bathroom, close to the beach. And the timing was so perfect, I had to say yes.

While living there I met my future husband and a few months later we decided to live together. Like magic, a little cabin became available on the property where he was leasing land and we took it. It had an outdoor shower, a daybed, mango trees, frangipani trees and so much more. So you see, I had to find the other place first before finding this place. My mind said "I want my perfect home now" but my heart guided me to take the other place first. Divine timing doesn't necessarily match the timing you have in mind.

In order to receive what you asked for, you have to learn to listen to your gut feeling, not your mind. You need to use your intuition, rather than your intellect. And this can be confusing at times. Because sometimes, you have so much input from your own mind and other people's minds, you don't even know how you feel about it anymore. Here are a few tips on how to listen to your own guidance system.

In the situation I just described, several people having several opinions about a decision you need to make, retreat. Be alone, go within, meditate. Ideally, meditate in nature. I have a spot here in Byron Bay that feels so clear and pure and raw, it's my place to gain clarity. There are no other people around so I can't possibly feel their energies and thoughts.

Another good method to gain clarity is the "2 second rule". Ask yourself "should I do xyz?" and answer straight away, from your gut feeling, not your mind, within 2 seconds. As soon as you start thinking about the answer you start analysing and weighing the pros and cons and in the end, you'll decide with your head, not your heart.

One thing that helped me a lot too were oracle cards. There's a ton of different cards you can use to get guidance. You can ask the angels and faeries and gods and goddesses. I have a few decks at home that I resonate with and when in doubt, I ask the cards. "What shall I do?" I thought, if I can't trust myself, I can trust the cards. Because the cards operate as my higher self. The card I pick is the card my higher self wants me to pick – no coincidences. I worked with tarot cards for a while too and thought it was a great way to tap into my subconscious.

Another method I have is to take any other person or thing or money out of the equation. Often we make decisions based on others or money. So ask yourself the question, "what would I do if money wasn't an issue?" That's how you find out what your heart really wants you to do. And if you decide based on that, money won't be an issue because you don't let it be an issue.

If you're already following your gut feeling most of the time and things still go wrong or don't happen exactly how you want them to happen, trust that it's part of the process. Often we have to learn a few things along the way, before we're ready to receive what we've asked for. Trust that you're always in the right place, at the right time, doing the right thing.

Exercise 1: sit in meditation for a few minutes. Close your eyes, take a few deep breaths and just be.

Exercise 2: Write down 10 things you're grateful for today.

Exercise 3: observe yourself when being asked to make a decision. Do you decide from your heart or your head? Be aware of it, then make steps towards changing it.

There's another brilliant Abraham Hicks Video on that topic. Go to YouTube and search for "Listen to your gut feeling!".

DAY
18

It's a very beautiful and sunny morning here in Byron Bay. A great day to be positive and attract even more positive things, people and circumstances into our lives.

You may have noticed your resistance towards some of the exercises. If not, great, you can go full steam ahead, nothing's stopping you from getting what you want. If you're like me, resistance does come up, sometimes even fear. So let's talk about how to identify this uncomfortable feeling as resistance or fear.

I find it hard sometimes to know when it's my gut feeling telling me "don't do it, it's not your path" and when it's fear telling me "don't do it, I'm so afraid". In most cases, I'm just afraid. A good indicator is when it's something that I used to say I would never do. Whenever I say "never" I can be sure I'll do it at some point in my life.

Let's look at fear for a moment. There's the fear that's very helpful to have. Like fear of falling down a cliff or being eaten by a bear. That fear of death or injury keeps us from doing stupid things. It's good that we feel it and then act accordingly.

And then there's another fear, one that most of us are dealing with. Fear of disapproval, fear of abandonment, fear of rejection, fear of being inappropriate, fear of being ridiculed, fear of being hurt, fear of judgment, fear of punishment, fear of failure and probably the biggest one, fear of success! How crazy is that? I love this quote by Marianne Williamson that really nails it:

"Our deepest fear is not that we are inadequate. Our deepest fear is that we are powerful beyond measure. It is our light, not our darkness that most frightens us."

Do we want to be stopped by fears like this? No way!

There's a book called "Feel the fear and do it anyway" by Susan Jeffers, I mentioned it earlier. I always liked the title and made it my motto. Only recently I read the book and one thing she says about fear is this:

Fear will always be there. It won't go away. The book isn't about "how to get rid of fear" it's about how to deal with fear. Whenever we do something that we haven't done before, there may be fear involved. Or maybe it's not as strong as fear but most likely we feel a bit uncomfortable, nervous, unsure. This is normal, we need to accept it and learn to live with it.

She also says that most fears come down to one basic fear: "What if I can't handle it?" That was a big "aha" moment for me and I looked at different fears and why we have them. And it's true, the underlying fear is always "what if I can't handle it?" We're not fearful of failure, we're fearful that we can't handle failure.

If you do have any fears that you think are holding you back from living the life you want, go through this exercise until you feel more comfortable:

Exercise 1: Make a list of all your fears. Then write behind every fear, "I can handle it." Anytime fear comes up, identify what you're afraid of and tell yourself "I can handle it."

I went on YouTube to find out how other people deal with fear and how they overcome it. And I came across this video, by a lady who's a rocket scientist. She grew up in poverty and managed to become a famous rocket scientist. And there was a lot of fear involved, as she tells in this TED talk.

She talks about 3 steps to overcoming fear:

1. You must name and reject your fear.

   And she doesn't mean it as in "ignore it" but reject it by saying "I'm afraid to fail but this won't stop me."

2. You must reprogram your brain with different thoughts.

   Tell yourself "I can do it". Learn everything you can about this thing you're afraid of.

3. You must rebuild your brain by taking action.

   She talks about taking action in opposition to your fear.

   If you want to watch this video, go to YouTube and search for "Reprogramming your brain to overcome fear".

We all deal with fear differently but I like her approach. "This won't stop me" is a very powerful statement to make. I use the words "I refuse" when I'm facing a situation where my mind's trying to manipulate me in moving forward. "I refuse to let this stop me."

Then, similar to what she describes, I tell my brain "you can do it". And if not now, maybe in a month or in a year. When you say "I can do it" the universe will respond and make sure that you can do it.

And yes, without action, nothing will happen. So baby step by baby step, I take action.

Hope you're having an empowering day everyone. Tell your fears that they won't stop you, it feels good!

Exercise 2: sit in meditation for a few minutes. Close your eyes, take a few deep breaths and just be.

Exercise 3: Write down 10 things you're grateful for today.

DAY
19

"Your vibe attracts your tribe."

—unkown

Good morning beautiful people. Hope you're still with us and enjoying yourselves. Meditating and writing isn't always convenient, I know. Most of us have such busy lives. I hope you all wrote "more time to play" on your lists? I did, long ago and I have a lot of time for myself. Thank you universe!

Have you shared this book with anyone? Your family, friends, work colleagues? Or would they not understand? I remember when I first started reading "spiritual" books. I would hide them because I didn't want anyone to judge me and laugh about me.

What you need - what we all need - is a support network. A group of people, or at least one person, who gets you. Someone who doesn't judge you but who supports and encourages you. Often, when we share our dreams with others, the reactions are "that's impossible", "as if it's that easy", "how are you going to do that?", "you're such a dreamer", "well, good luck then". Then they continue to give you "good advice" and remind you that "life's hard" and "money doesn't grow on trees". You can try to explain to them the law of attraction and the power of intention, they won't believe it. Even if you show them scientific proof - which now exists - they still push it away, labeling it "aerie faerie" or "woo woo" or worse.

And you know what that is? Fear. They're fearful of the unknown so they laugh about it and reject it. And reject you because you're into all this "stuff". We've probably all experienced something along those lines and have become a bit protective about our dreams. We don't want to risk anyone crushing them with one stupid remark. So we keep our precious dreams to ourselves until we feel confident enough about it to tell the world.

So until you've found this confidence and knowing that you'll have all the things you've asked for, be selective about who you share your dreams with. Find like-minded people, spend time with fellow dreamers. And if you feel like you don't have like-minded people around you, you can ask for them to come into your life.

Having this friend or group of friends that you can dream with and get excited about it with is a bit like being part of a secret society. "The others" don't understand, they live in their "life's hard" competitive world. But you, you live in a world where anything is possible and your dreams won't stay dreams forever, they become a reality.

So today, if you haven't done so already, identify the people you feel safe to share your thoughts on manifesting with. Find out who your fellow dreamers are, those people you can trust and share your "secret" with.

Once you've identified your "tribe", think about why you love and admire them. I have friends that I admire for their courage and strength, friends I admire for their relationships, their focus in business, their surfing skills, their positive mindset, the way they are with their children etc. So if I want to become a better surfer, of course I'll seek advice from my amazing surfer friend. You don't ask somebody who's broke about abundance and you don't ask someone who's fearful of leaving their comfort zone about leaving your comfort zone. So have the right conversations with the right people.

I found a very helpful video by Mastin Kipp. Go to YouTube and search for "How to find your soul tribe." Enjoy!

Exercise 1: sit in meditation for a few minutes. Close your eyes, take a few deep breaths and just be.

Exercise 2: Write down 10 things you're grateful for today.

Exercise 3: Find your soul tribe! Look around you, are your friends supporting you or are they bringing you down? Be selective about who you spend your time with and who you ask for specific advice.

DAY
20

"Many of life's failures are people who did not realize how close they were to success when they gave up."

—Thomas A. Edison

Good morning day 20. We've been doing this for almost 3 weeks now so we've almost created a new habit. Did you know that it takes 21 days to create a new habit? That also means, that it only takes 21 days to un-create an old, unhealthy habit. But there's one thing that a lot of people find challenging. You need to be persistent.

The official definition of 'persistence' is:" the fact of continuing in an opinion or course of action in spite of difficulty or opposition." It means that even if you find it hard and resist it, you just do it!

We don't like to hear words like persistence, discipline, consistency or focus. It means we need to get our butt off the couch and do something. Everyone who's tried to lose weight knows that it requires all these things to successfully lose weight and keep it off. And it's the same with developing a new spiritual practice or belief.

In the spiritual community it's often talked about going with the flow, not forcing anything, surrendering to what is, letting go. And that's all good - as long as you don't use it as an excuse for being lazy and not doing the work.

I'm quite good with discipline and staying focused. I'm used to motivating myself because I've been working from home for over 6 years. And I realised very quickly that if I don't do my work, the only person that's losing is me. And why would I let myself down in that way? So think about it, if you don't do it, you're only letting yourself down, no one else. The gratitude practice, the meditation, the positive thinking - you're not doing this for me because I've gone through the effort of writing it all up, you're doing it for you and you're doing it of your own free will.

So here's what helps me to stay focused and be persistent with a practice that I'd like to incorporate into my life.

1. Don't set your goals too high.

I mentioned at the beginning, if a 20-minute meditation is too hard to do, try 15 or 10 or 5. Come on, you can do 5! It's supposed to be fun and easy because if it's not, you'll stop trying. It's so rewarding to achieve your goals, no matter how small they are. You're much more likely to continue and maybe even increase the time you're meditating for if you set yourself a realistic goal that's easily achievable.

2. Make time for your new habit or practice.

When I find myself repeatedly prioritising work over my new project or practice I make appointments in my calendar, just like I do for work appointments. I would for example block one hour each morning to meditate and write down the things I'm grateful for. Then I'd start my workday and I also make sure that I finish on time. There's always more work, don't attempt to do it all in one day.

3. Ask for help.

If you're having trouble staying focused and feel like you're constantly manipulating yourself, ask for help! Join a program online or a local support group. Or do what I did, find an "accountability partner". Meet with them every 2 weeks and set some goals. Then report back to them how you went. It's good for two reasons. 1. You're getting clear on what you want and 2. you're more likely to do your "homework" because somebody will ask you about it. You can't hide, you have someone there who will remind you of your commitment.

I'm sure there are more ways, but these are my most successful ones. Having you read my blog makes me stay focused and write every day. There's no slacking off when you have an audience.

If you're not able to develop a regular practice, it's important not to beat yourself up about it. Don't go into negative self-talk and call yourself "useless" or anything else along those lines. Continue to practice self-love and congratulate yourself for at least having tried. And then, when you feel ready, you'll just try again. Because if you really want something, it'll creep back into your mind and you'll try again and again and again.

And look at why you can't stay focused or commit to something. Is this a pattern of yours? Why are you sabotaging yourself? Are you used to not getting what you want? Do you think you're not worthy of having what you want? Instead of seeing it as failure, see it as something you need to learn from.

There's a very interesting video about "The 4 Ways to Successfully Adopt New Habits" by Gretchen Rubin on YouTube.

Starting a new habit means setting a new rule for ourselves. And we all respond very differently to rules, both external and internal rules. Knowing a bit more about how you react to rules may be helpful to successfully start a new habit. It helped me a lot!

Exercise 1: sit in meditation for a few minutes. Close your eyes, take a few deep breaths and just be.

Exercise 2: Write down 10 things you're grateful for today.

Exercise 3: look at how successful or unsuccessful you are at implementing new habits. Is it easy or are you struggling? Maybe it's got to do with how you respond to rules? Watch the video to gain clarity on this one. If you don't want to watch it because I said so, you may fall into the category "the Rebel".

DAY
21

"Remember to celebrate the little things."

—unknown

Today's celebration day! Not just because it's Friday, the end of the workweek for some of us, but because we don't celebrate enough. Don't forget to celebrate your achievements, as small as they may be. And if you feel like there's nothing to celebrate, just celebrate life. The fact that you're here, you're healthy and doing the best you can.

The good thing about writing wish lists is that you can go back to them and re-read them. When you make a wish list in your head, you often forget what was on there. And when you receive what you asked for, you can't even remember ever asking for it. You just take it for granted.

I remember a friend of mine saying that she had been dreaming of living by the ocean for years. And she did manage to live by the ocean! But she just kept living her life with all its problems and challenges. And after a few years she didn't pay much attention to the ocean anymore. And then it dawned to her that she had received exactly what she had asked for. She looked back at her life and realised how far she had come and how much she had achieved.

Sometimes we don't even realise that we got what we wanted. If for example you're asking for "more time to do what I love" or "more freedom", it can mean that you'll lose your job. And you see it as something negative but you got what you wanted, a lot of spare time. We just tend to panic and think we'll never find work again and run out of money. But we always find work and we're always looked after. When was the last time that you had nothing to eat on your table?

Other times, we don't even ask for more time. But we ask to launch a book for example and we may think we can write after work or on the weekends. But the universe has a different idea, it wants us to make it a priority. That happened to me. 2 clients of mine left because they had decided to work with an agency who can look after all their marketing rather than having lots of individual service providers. And when they did, I was kind of relieved. And I even let another client go because I realised I needed more time.

So every step along the way, no matter how insignificant you think it is, is worth celebrating. Even moments that you think are disastrous, like losing a job, are worth celebrating. Since you're always at the right place, at the right time, doing the right thing, it MUST be for your benefit.

So today, celebrate how far you've come. You can go back to your list and see if there's anything you've made progress with. Maybe you can even tick off a few things. I can tick off "dark blue Subaru

Forester". I've wanted this car for 2 years but wasn't attached to when this was going to happen. I happily drove my little old car in the meantime and was grateful for it every day. I was very specific about what I wanted - dark blue, under 150,000 kms, manual, registered in NSW, under $10,000. And one day, there it was. I was the first person to see it, I had the money, and it all flowed.

I have a friend who would call up and say "let's celebrate." And I would ask, "What are we celebrating?". "Nothing specific", she would say, "just life." And we'd go for dinner or cocktails or to the beach, whatever celebrating means to us in that moment. It feels very special and it's so much fun!

Exercise 1: sit in meditation for a few minutes. Close your eyes, take a few deep breaths and just be.

Exercise 2: Write down 10 things you're grateful for today.

Exercise 3: give yourself a pat on the back and say "well done". Have a celebration with yourself or friends, just to honour how far you've come and be grateful for all the people, things and circumstances you've attracted into your life so far.

DAY
22

"Whatever makes you uncomfortable is your biggest opportunity for growth."

—Bryant McGill

Today's topic was inspired by my husband, who suggested that in order to make your dreams come true, you should spend a day the way you imagine your new life to be and see if you feel comfortable with this new lifestyle.

If you wish to have less work, less stress, less things to do - take a day off work or use a weekend to do nothing, or do less. Do you feel anxious about doing nothing? Do you lie on the beach thinking about the emails you need to write and the house you need to clean? From a point of discomfort, anxiety and guilt, you can only attract more discomfort, anxiety and guilt.

It doesn't mean the life you want is not for you, it just means that you've got a bit of work to do until you can live that life and feel good about it. We often ask for big changes and we want them right now. But be careful what you're asking for, big changes can be scary. So accept that it takes some time to get to where you want to be. Remember, time is helping you, it's not working against you.

When I quit my job and became self-employed, everybody assumed that I had more time and more flexibility and that I had "made it". But I was so used to working 9 to 5, I just kept working 9 to 5. And I was so used to going to an office, I didn't mind to work at my clients' offices. I was still stressed and couldn't enjoy my new freedom.

Slowly but surely I settled into my new lifestyle and started making space for things other than my work. When I moved to Byron I went from an 8 hour down to a 6-hour day and thought I had "made it". Then down to 4 hours, now I work occasionally.

So rather than wanting everything all at once, practice patience. When we talked about 'visualising' I suggested you take your dream car for a test drive. And I'd suggest you take your dream lifestyle for a test drive too and see if you get along. And if it doesn't feel comfortable, just start smaller and work your way up.

Exercise 1: sit in meditation for a few minutes. Close your eyes, take a few deep breaths and just be.

Exercise 2: Write down 10 things you're grateful for today.

Exercise 3: Test-drive your dreams. This doesn't need to happen today, but do make sure to make time to try out your new life and see if it feels good. If it's too much too soon, take baby steps.

DAY
23

"The way you treat yourself sets the standard for others."

—Dr. Sonya Friedman

Good morning everyone, did you wake up with good thoughts today? I just wrote down in my journal how grateful I am to be waking up happy every morning. The way we start our day is how we live our life, some wise person once said. I have to agree.

Today we're going to talk about self-love. Something that a lot of us tend to neglect. In our society we're told to love others more than ourselves, to put everyone else first, to please others. Putting yourself first is often seen as being selfish. I can tell you, it's not.

Remember the oxygen masks on the planes? Put on your mask first before helping others to put on theirs. If we have no energy, how can we possibly give to others? That's why it's so important for mothers especially to take some time to recharge their batteries. It's much easier to give to your children if you feel great and energised.

How does loving yourself and putting yourself first relate to manifesting? It's a big part of it. If you love yourself, you feel worthy. And in order to receive all the things, people and circumstances you're dreaming of, you need to know that you're worthy of having them.

People with low self-esteem have trouble manifesting what they want because they don't think they deserve good things. How you feel about yourself will always be reflected back to you. When you think you're not good enough, the universe will respond by not giving you what you want.

Most of us probably wrote "great relationships" or "great friends" or the "dream partner" on our list. And the same principle that I just described applies to people. They can only love you as much as you can love yourself. So if you want to improve your existing relationship or attract a new one, all you need to do is love yourself more.

The good news is, you don't need to try and change anyone or change the things on your list, you just need to work on yourself. It can be confronting at first, especially if you've believed your whole life that you're not that great. But it gets easier with time and it can be fun to watch how all your relationships are getting better and better.

That can mean that some relationships are no longer possible. If you've been a victim your whole life and you had a friend who treated you like one that friendship won't work anymore. If you have a friend who doesn't have any self-respect but you do, it'll be difficult to maintain this friendship. You may just see these people less and less and new friends who will be a reflection of the new you will come into your life

The first tip I'd like to give you is: watch your thoughts. How are you talking to yourself? "Silly me", "I'm such an idiot", "I'm useless"? Or "well done", "you're amazing", "you're a genius", "I'm the best cook, I love my own food". Stop being mean to yourself. Instead, praise yourself, applaud yourself, and tell yourself how amazing you are.

My second tip is, use positive affirmations and repeat them as often as you need to. Repeat them until you believe them. If you feel undeserving, a good one is "I deserve to be happy", "I deserve to have great relationships", "I deserve ..." fill in the gap. Once you feel comfortable with it, try something bigger. "I deserve to take a year off and just travel and go with the flow." Yes you do! We all do.

And tip number 3 is, treat yourself the way you want to be treated. Have a massage, go to the sauna, buy yourself some nice things, and treat yourself to a nice lunch or a wellness weekend. Nurture yourself! If you feel down and sad, don't have a drink, have a healing massage instead. Don't take up smoking again, go to the farmers market and buy yourself some nice organic food. Treat yourself with love and respect.

If you're loving and kind to yourself, others will treat you in the same way. "She always cuts me off." or "He never listens." Does that sound familiar? Watch them change as you change. They won't do it anymore if you feel you deserve to finish your sentence or to have somebody's full attention when you talk to them.

Exercise 1: sit in meditation for a few minutes. Close your eyes, take a few deep breaths and just be.

Exercise 2: Write down 10 things you're grateful for today.

Exercise 3: Watch your thoughts and change negative into positive self-talk. Use positive affirmations and tell yourself over and over again "I am deserving". Act like you love yourself, give yourself nice presents, pamper yourself, and spend some quality time with yourself.

And go to YouTube to watch this video of self-love guru "Louise Hay - Loving Yourself."

DAY
24

"Blessed is he who has learned to admire but not envy, to follow but not imitate, to praise but not flatter, and to lead but not manipulate."

—William Arthur Ward

One more week to go! Which doesn't mean it's over, we're only getting started! With all the tools you'll have by the end of this month, you should be well prepared for the future. We all have to continue to train our minds, to let go of past beliefs and visualise the life we want to live.

Today we'll talk about a subject that's important to consider when manifesting - jealousy, envy, resentment. You may have guessed it, these emotions aren't helping you, and they're making it hard for you to manifest the things you want.

We sometimes say "Oh, I'm so jealous" when somebody tells us about an upcoming holiday for example. Shouldn't we instead say, "Oh, I'm so happy for you!"? Being jealous or envious is a very low vibration. By saying we're jealous, we're saying that we want what they have but we don't think we can have it. Being jealous of somebody's life is disempowering, being inspired by somebody's life is empowering.

Even worse is a feeling of resentment, which is defined as "bitter indignation at having been treated unfairly." When you have resentment, you often blame others for not having what you want and you put yourself in the position of the victim. "It's so unfair".

I had a friend who wanted a boyfriend but she always said "I hate seeing happy couples." She obviously didn't know about the law of attraction and the fact that what you put out, you attract. By looking at them with envy and a feeling of lack, we'll attract more lack. How do we expect to be in a happy relationship when we hate to see happy couples? Instead of hating them, we should seek their company. Hang out with your happy couple friends and feel how it feels to be happy with someone if you want to attract a healthy partnership.

People also talk about someone being "filthy rich". As if being rich is something bad. Yet they want to be rich themselves. When you talk about money in a negative way it's a clear sign for the universe not to give you any - because you don't seem to like it! So again, be careful how you label things.

I believe that what people really think when they say "I'm jealous" is "it's so unfair, how come she's so successful? I'm just as talented as she is. Yet she's made it and I haven't. How does she do it?" I can tell you how she does it, she's just better at manifesting. She knows what she wants, she believes she can have it, she's open to let it come to her. And she probably has so much gratitude for what she has so she's attracting more and more success into her life.

Tip 1: don't say you're jealous, say you're happy for the other person. Don't be a victim, be inspired by what the other person has achieved and know that if she can do it, you can do it too.

Tip 2: spend more time with these people. Find out how they do it. Ask them, "How did you do it?" Try to learn from them rather than being jealous of them.

Exercise 1: sit in meditation for a few minutes. Close your eyes, take a few deep breaths and just be.

Exercise 2: Write down 10 things you're grateful for today.

Exercise 3: whenever you catch yourself being jealous or envious of someone, change this feeling into a positive one. Admire this person, be inspired by this person, and know that if he or she can do it, you can too.

You'll find another inspiring video by Abraham Hicks on YouTube: "How to deal with jealousy". Enjoy!

DAY
25

"May what I do flow from me like a river, no forcing and no holding back, the way it is with children."

—Rainer Maria Rilke

Is everything flowing for you? Do you think "life is easy"? and "everything comes to me with ease?" I hope you do because that's another secret to manifesting, EASE and FLOW.

Too often we push towards our dreams and goals and pushing isn't being in the flow. It's trying to redirect the flow or speed up the flow or try to have a peak into the future and see where the flow's taking you. Pushing is trying to control. Yet we are taught that sometimes you just need to push. Don't you hate being pushed? Do you think the flow likes to be pushed?

Once we've gotten clear about what we want we often want to have it right now. And sure, once we create it with our mind, we already have it. Not in our physical experience, yes. But it's not up to us to decide and control when this is happening, that's up to the universe. It'll happen in divine timing.

I'll give you an example. Let's say you want to travel the world but you don't have the funds at the moment. You're trying to put money aside, you don't eat out anymore, you don't go shopping, and you do everything you can to save up some extra dollars to go traveling. Then your car breaks down, or you receive a letter from the tax office, or some other big expense comes up. And you protest and you get angry and upset that the money you saved for your holiday is gone again.

Instead, accept it and move on. And see it as a sign that you're not meant to go on this trip right now. There are things you need to learn before you can head off, things you need to do. Pushing to go on this holiday isn't in the flow and it's obviously not easy for you at the moment. So postpone it until the funds materialise with ease.

And I can tell you how funds can materialise with ease. Last year I received an email from someone asking if I could do some work for them. It seemed like they knew me so I did a bit of research and found out that I had done some work for them 4 years ago. They needed about 10 hours of my time to help them set up some AdWords accounts. Nice, an extra 10 hours were just what I needed because I was going to Germany and didn't mind some extra cash. A week later they called and asked me "how many hours do we get for $6,500?" I told them and they said "ok, we'd like to pay you right now." It was the end of the financial year and they wanted to make sure to spend that money before the end of June. When I didn't send the invoice straight away they reminded me, "Could you please send the invoice? We'd like to pay you." I liked the sound of that!

So there were my funds, more than I asked for! It was so easy and I didn't have to do anything! I didn't have to ask for more work, I didn't have to discuss my hourly rate with anyone, I didn't have to change the way I work. It was just handed to me. I worked off the hours over time and that was easy enough.

"But" you may say, "I can't just sit around and do nothing!" Yes you can. And you're never doing nothing. First of all, you're thinking, that's doing something. And you're visualising and you're feeling how it feels to be where you want to be. If there's a need for action it'll be very obvious. But don't get stuck on what that action should be. Leave it up to the universe to show you the steps.

We like to figure things out. We know where we want to be so we start planning. We want to know all the steps to get there and once we're satisfied with our plan we start to action it. And we're so disappointed when something goes wrong. We assume that since this step went wrong, we can't have what we want! Because we think it's the only way to get there. But there are so many different ways to get there, we can't possibly know them all.

I'll give you another example. A friend of mine, an architect, lived with me in Sydney for a while. She wanted to work as an architect but it didn't flow so she started working at a cafe around the corner. That was the easy option and it was flowing very nicely. Then one day, a customer told her that he was stressed because he had just lost an architect from his team. "I'm an architect" she said. Long story short, she started working for him. Who would have thought that she would find a job as an architect by working as a waitress?

And that's the thing, we can't figure it out so we may as well go with the flow and go with what's easy. If something doesn't come with ease, it's not the right time. Some call it "the path of least resistance".

Exercise 1: sit in meditation for a few minutes. Close your eyes, take a few deep breaths and just be.

Exercise 2: Write down 10 things you're grateful for today.

Exercise 3: whatever you do, ask yourself. Is it easy? Am I in the flow? If you're banging your head against the wall, stop doing what you're doing and try something else.

There's a great video on YouTube by Abraham Hicks about "Ease and Flow".

DAY
26

"Service to others is the rent you pay for your room here on earth."

—Muhammad Ali

Good afternoon! I had a busy morning and needed to prioritise other stuff. Has this happened to you before? Did you forget to do your gratitude practice? Did life just get in the way? That's normal and breaking our routine is healthy. And when we've had a break, we can go back to it, hopefully with some renewed enthusiasm.

Today's topic is "being of service". I had a discussion with a friend about this once and she said she didn't like the expression, "being of service". It sounded like being a servant, being obedient, needing to do something in order to "deserve" something. And I get it, to me it also felt a bit like selflessly serving your master. It didn't sound empowering to me.

But I've since changed my opinion and discovered a different way of interpreting "being of service". To me it simply means, doing something good, trying your best, wanting to help, wanting to improve the state our environment is in, caring about others, wanting the best outcome for everyone, being willing to do your part, spreading the love.

What does it have to do with manifesting? I've mentioned it before, if we want something for the wrong reasons, it won't come easily, maybe not at all. If I wanted to write a book to make money, that wouldn't be a good reason. Or if I wanted to write a book to impress someone, that wouldn't be a good reason either.

But if I wanted to write a book to help others and to inspire others, that would be a very good reason. That's what being of service means.

Being of service doesn't mean to selflessly dedicate your life to other people though. You're not asked to put yourself last. No, you need to do it because you love it and the fact that it benefits someone else is part of why you love it.

To stay with the writing example. I don't just do it because it makes me happy to help others. I also do it simply because I have the urge to write. Writing is my creative outlet, it makes me happy and my life feels in balance when I'm expressing my creativity through words.

And I'll give you another example, hotels. If you look at successful hotels and ask the owner why they created it, they won't say, "Because I wanted to make money". Most likely they'll say they love seeing their guests happy. A lot of them will also tell you they love interior design and have an attention to detail. They love staying in nice hotels themselves and enjoy a nice atmosphere, good food and a cozy bed. They love creating a home away from home and to make people feel comfortable. I just spoke to someone who's renting out cozy cabins to honeymooners and he said "oh, we just love to spoil our guests. Most of them become friends of ours." He clearly loved his job and yes, he loved being of service.

It's really important to do something you love and to do something that in some way or another enriches people's lives. Some of us make beautiful art, others are bus drivers. I actually met a bus driver once who told me that he loved his job and that he always meets such nice people. He was of service and loving it.

But it's not necessarily about being of service to other humans. Some people are standing up for animal rights or are of service to planet Earth. They are fulfilled when they know they can save marine life or find better ways to produce energy.

I have two friends who have both created vegan make up brands and aside from running their businesses they spend a lot of time and energy to educate people about the mistreatment of animals in the cosmetic industry and encourage others to stand up for those who don't have a voice (a human voice).

So ask yourself, "how can I be of service?" Enjoying what you do and helping others at the same time is where you want to be. The universe loves that.

Exercise 1: sit in meditation for a few minutes. Close your eyes, take a few deep breaths and just be.

Exercise 2: Write down 10 things you're grateful for today.

Exercise 3: ask yourself, how can I be of service? Live from a place of love, not fear. Don't think about making money all the time, the money will come if you're loving what you're doing and if you're of service to others.

DAY
27

"When you learn not to want things so badly, life comes to you."

—Jessica Lange

4 days to go until Magical May is over, are you sad? The good news is, after May comes June and you can make June magical too. It's your choice how you experience life so choose next month to be amazing too. "Joyful June" maybe?

I've mentioned many times how important it is to be grateful for what you have but I'd like to talk about it again, in a bit more detail. In order to attract the things you want in your life it's important to appreciate what you have right now.

I once watched a YouTube video about a super successful woman who was a guest in a talk show. She had grown up in one of the poorest communities of the city she lived in. "How could she have become so successful, living in poverty?" You may ask. And that's what the host of the talk show asked her too.

She explained that growing up, her mother always told her that they had everything they needed and that she should be grateful for what she had. And she believed it. Of course the kids at school would tell her otherwise but her mum's voice was stronger. She was also told that she could be whoever she wanted, have whatever job she wanted. To the outside world she lived a life of lack but her inner world was one of abundance, with no limitations.

And then we listen to ourselves sometimes, how we're complaining about things that are of no importance. I like the expression "first world problems". We don't have problems like having no food to eat or no place to sleep, we obsess about things like our flight being delayed or not finding a parking spot or our hips being too big. Who cares? It's not the end of the world.

Instead of being stressed about these "first world problems", let's appreciate what we have right now.

When Andy and I moved into the cabin we started getting drinking water from town because we didn't want to drink unfiltered rainwater. At first I noticed how often I went to get water and it was an extra task on my to do list. But after a while I got so used to it, I didn't even notice anymore. I was just happy to have a constant supply of fresh drinking water.

For the new home we bought a very advanced rainwater filter system. It's very convenient but I didn't jump up and down and said "Finally, I don't have to go into town anymore to get that stupid water." I didn't mind at all and if I didn't have the new filter, I'd be happy too.

Another example is my new car. I was so happy with my old car and often said how grateful I was for the car to be so reliable. I never said "I can't wait to get rid of this shitty old car." I bet the new car wouldn't have come with so much ease if I had been annoyed and ungrateful for the car I had before.

When we appreciate what we have, we're not so desperate to get something else or something better. We allow it to come in naturally because we're detached from it. We're not in need of it.

The combination of appreciation and detachment is ideal. If we're attached to an outcome and it doesn't happen as expected, it'll be a big drama! But if we're detached from the outcome, whatever happens will be fine.

This isn't new but I'll repeat it again: the more we appreciate things, the more things we will receive to be appreciative of. And vice versa. That's why the gratitude practice is so powerful. It gets us out of our complaining, wanting things to be different, wanting to have more and brings us back into alignment with a feeling of contentment. And from that feeling we can attract all the beautiful things we want to have.

Abraham Hicks talks about "Appreciation without attachment" in this YouTube video.

And what's important here too and I can't say it often enough: Your outer world reflects your inner world. If you're not appreciative of your outer world, ask yourself "am I appreciating myself?" Love yourself and everything else will fall into place.

Exercise 1: sit in meditation for a few minutes. Close your eyes, take a few deep breaths and just be.

Exercise 2: Write down 10 things you're grateful for today.

Exercise 3: appreciate what you have. Know what you want but detach from the outcome. Be happy now! Because your point of attraction is the present moment. And make sure you appreciate yourself, that's very important.

DAY
28

"All the suffering, stress, and addiction comes from not realizing you already are what you are looking for."

—Jon Kabat-Zinn

It's the weekend, yay! Have you had a few beers last night? And are you having a strong coffee this morning to wake up? Have you ever thought about drugs clouding your vision? That's what we're talking about today, drugs.

You may want to protest, "alcohol is not a drug" or "coffee is not a drug". They are, and so is sugar. When somebody says "drugs" we straight away think heroin or cocaine. Of course, we don't want to admit that we're all taking drugs. Let's look at the definition of drugs:

noun: "a medicine or other substance which has a physiological effect when ingested or otherwise introduced into the body."

verb: "administer a drug to (someone) in order to induce stupor or insensibility."

Two things stand out for me "has a physiological effect" and "induce stupor or insensibility".

We talked about listening to our intuition or our gut feeling a few days ago. In order to listen we need to have a clear and receptive mind. Now how do we feel when we have a hangover? Have you heard the expression "brain fog"? It's not an official word but I found a good definition by a doctor. He says "may be described as feelings of mental confusion or lack of mental clarity".

Isn't that the exact opposite of how we want to feel? We want clarity, not confusion.

So consider dropping some of those unhealthy habits if you have a feeling that they make you less sensitive to your own guidance.

I quit cigarettes when I was 28 - some of my "new" friends can't even imagine that I used to smoke! Then I drank less and less alcohol. I didn't plan it but it just happened that all my friends were overseas and it was winter and I just didn't go out. When I went to a party a month later I couldn't handle more than a beer. And then I decided I don't need this stuff anymore. It didn't make me feel good, it made me feel terrible and dehydrated and I didn't sleep well.

The next substance I had to cut out was coffee. I felt good on it but I felt terrible off it. I only had a cup per day but it was enough for me to get hooked. If I didn't have my coffee for just one day, I got the worst migraines. So I quit. I went back to it once and the first coffee felt like some heavy drug. My mind was busy and I felt anxious.

I'm also eating less sugar and no refined sugar at all if possible. Same thing, if I buy chocolate, I'll eat it and I want to eat it again the next day. If I don't buy it, I don't miss it. My teeth got so sensitive, they hurt if I eat too much sugar. Has anyone of you seen the picture of the brain of a cocaine addict and the brain of a sugar addict? Google it! You'll find that there are a lot of similarities, it's quite disturbing.

The problem with these drugs is that they're not only accepted in our society, it's considered "normal" to take them. You're a weirdo if you don't want cake and people call you "boring" when you say "no" to alcohol. It can make you feel like an outsider not to drink alcohol or coffee because any social event involves either.

At first this may be the case but remember what I talked about a few days ago, finding your tribe. There are people who are not into drugs and who understand that your intuition works much better when you're not feeling foggy all the time. Actually, the intuition doesn't work better, you just become a much better listener when you're sober.

Now don't feel bad and beat yourself up if you're still drinking coffee and enjoying your cake with it. And understand that cutting it all out may take a few years because you don't want to force it, you want it to happen naturally. (Remember, no pushing, instead, go with the flow.)

The important message here is that it's a fact that any kind of drugs, whether socially acceptable or not, numb your senses. So consider not taking some substances if you want to be sensitive to your own guidance.

Exercise 1: sit in meditation for a few minutes. Close your eyes, take a few deep breaths and just be.

Exercise 2: Write down 10 things you're grateful for today.

Exercise 3: look at your eating and drinking habits (and smoking habits if you're a smoker). Have you become reliant on any substance? Is there anything in particular that you feel is numbing your senses? Consider reducing it or cutting it out completely.

DAY
29

"Don't let your fear of being judged stop you from asking for help when you need it."

—Unknown

I've gone through my repertoire of things that helped me manifest again and found another big one. Whenever I feel that I'm really stuck and my will power doesn't get me out of this stuckness, I ask for help.

I have a few trusted healers in the area and I've also met some amazing healers while traveling or living overseas. When I talk about healers I'm referring to what most people call "spiritual healers" and body workers.

When I realised that the different parts of our body relate to certain emotions, I started observing where I hold tension and then read about what it related to. I noticed a pattern and I also noticed that some of the stuff was old, very old.

Just by being aware of what's causing tension or pain in your body can help to release it and you can do certain exercises to work on it yourself. But often, blocks can only be released with the help of another person. For me, massages are great. When the physical tension is worked on the emotions that are related to it automatically release as well.

If you're having trouble with your inner organs, you may want to consult with a naturopath, Chinese herbalist, acupuncturist or similar. I don't know about your experience with doctors but I found that they never try to get to the source of the problem, they just give you something to work on the effects. And that only provides a temporary relief. Which is why some people are put on medication for their whole lives. Their emotions are not healed, just numbed.

Another modality I love is any form of energy healing. A lot of you may have heard of Reiki but there's probably as many different methods as there are people on the planet. It gently releases blocks, conscious and subconscious. And that's what I find happens a lot, that I'm not even aware where the source of the issue is.

I recently went to a healer and told her I needed help to get ready to receive all that I've asked for. I felt like there was still some resistance but I had no idea where it was coming from. She traced some of it back to my early childhood, fascinating! Especially because my mind wasn't holding these old beliefs anymore, I had cleared them a long time ago. But my body was still holding them, there were still some old patterns present in my energy.

What's important to understand about healers is that they're not more powerful than you are. They've just developed a skill that you don't have. And they rely on you to cooperate and be open to receive the healing.

A healer is a facilitator who helps you heal yourself. Because if you're not open to healing, it won't work. You're using your own healing powers and what we call "source energy" which is available to all of us. The healer knows how to draw from this source energy and direct it to you.

Healing works through intention. The healer has the intention to help, you have the intention to be helped and the universe does the rest.

I'm just mentioning it because too often, people worship healers and put them on a pedestal. They like to give all their power away to the healer and become dependent on him. So stay in your power, know that healing is a co-creation between you, the healer and source energy.

Healing can also occur in certain places and a lot of people, who want to better their lives, seek out these places. A lot of temples and churches have been built on energetically powerful places and whether you're religious or not, you can instantly feel it when entering such a place. I've had amazing experiences and deep healing occur in churches and ancient temples. Just stand on top of a mountain, that'll charge you up and release a lot of stuff from your system. You just need to be open to it and believe in it.

Exercise 1: sit in meditation for a few minutes. Close your eyes, take a few deep breaths and just be.

Exercise 2: Write down 10 things you're grateful for today.

Exercise 3: do you need support in releasing blocks so you can move forward in life? Do some research, find a healing method that resonates with you. The key is to really feel a full body "Yes" for a place or specific healer. Don't do it if you're hesitant, that means you're not fully open and ready.

DAY
30

"Writing is a way of processing our lives. And it can be a way of healing."

—Jan Karon

Good morning my lovely readers. Thanks so much for your support over the last 30 days. Your feedback means the world to me! I'm getting a bit sentimental, only one more day. After that I hope you feel more clear about how to manifest the life of your dreams and have identified the areas in your life that you still need to work on. For me, the end of May won't mean the end of writing, I'm only getting started. June will be dedicated to making all theses posts into a book.

And I'd like to share the last helpful tool with you, WRITING. At the beginning of the month I asked you to write down what you would like to create in your life. And I've asked you to write down 10 things that you are grateful for every day. I didn't do this to give you extra homework, I did it knowing that writing it down will make it more powerful and will bring clarity.

The good thing about writing is, you can always go back to it later and add to it or change it. Once a thought is gone, it's often gone forever. I used to keep my journals for a year or two and sometimes open them and start reading. I made a few interesting observations doing that.

1. A lot of the things that I had wanted had come into my life. That helped me see that I AM a great manifestor.
2. I realised how far I had come. Shouldn't that be celebrated? It made me realise that I was always looking to the future, never stopping and being grateful for where I was right now.
3. I noticed patterns in my thinking and behavior. Gosh, I had some obsessive thinking going on! Stressing and worrying about details that a month down the track didn't matter anymore. Great to detect these patterns and work on releasing them.

Writing is great for deep self-reflection. But you can only go deep if you're brutally honest with yourself. Don't hold back, your journal is for your eyes only. You can accuse people of being a b**ch or an a**hole and all sorts of other stuff. No one will judge you.

You can rant about how annoying and unfair life is, you can talk about feelings of insecurity and hatred and anxiety. Get it off your chest! Or your mind. In Germany we say "to get it off your soul".

The aim is not to write a beautiful piece of poetry, it's to process stuff that's going on inside you and that may be so ridiculous in your eyes, you don't even want to share it with your best friend. Because you don't want to bother them and use them as a doormat. Understandable!

And as I mentioned before, nobody wants to hang out with people who complain all the time. Sure, it's fine to have a good cry on somebody's shoulder but we don't want to abuse our friends as therapists. I was always someone to process it first, then meet my friends with renewed optimism. It's not worth using the precious time you have with someone to talk about life's dramas and create more drama in the process! If you still feel like sharing your thoughts with a person, not just your journal, seek out professional help.

But a journal isn't just for your complaints and worries, it's also for your gratitude and the amazing things that are happening in your life.

Sometimes my journal reads like this. "Oh my god, I can't believe how good I feel. Everything's just flowing and I'm receiving good news every day." Over time you may see a change in what you're writing about. No more worrying about money, no more issues with friends or colleagues and instead, a lot of things to be grateful for.

My recommendation for all of you is to get a journal. And once you've filled it, read it or burn it, do whatever you like with it. As I said, reflection can be helpful but sometimes the writing in itself is enough for you to let it go. Let the words flow onto the page and out of your mind, no need to revisit if it feels like completion to you.

I knew someone who had trouble writing so she started by writing just one word. I couldn't relate to that, I could write forever! But if you do have a resistance to writing, start small. Just like with the meditation, start with an amount that doesn't feel overwhelming.

Exercise 1: sit in meditation for a few minutes. Close your eyes, take a few deep breaths and just be.

Exercise 2: Write down 10 things you're grateful for today.

Exercise 3: get a journal and start writing - about the things you want, how you feel, what moves you. Don't hold back, it's for your eyes only. Do you feel lighter after you've gotten something off your chest? Use the process of writing to get clear on what you want and to release any blocks you may have towards moving forward.

DAY
31

Good morning magical ones. The last day of May and the end of "Magical May". Hope you all enjoyed it and learned everything you need to know about manifesting. You probably learned a lot about yourself and your beliefs. And realised that all those people who "made it" weren't just lucky. They knew what they wanted and were open to receive it!

Opening up to receiving and believing that it's coming is the biggest challenge and requires a lot of time, energy and patience. Like Louise Hay said, "it's simple, but it's not always easy".

To summarise what the keys to a happy life are, I would say being clear about what you want is the most important thing. If we change our mind all the time we're sending mixed messages and the universe will have trouble to deliver it to us. Did you want the green or the red car? You need to decide!

Visualising your desires and feeling how it feels to have them is usually quite easy and it's fun too. Do it often!

Knowing you're worthy of it and trusting that it's coming is what most of us still need to work on. Do anything it takes. Write, watch your thought patterns and change them, surround yourself with positive people, give yourself the love you want others to give you, seek out healers to help you move through your blocks.

And celebrate your successes, even the smallest ones. Give thanks for what you have right now, don't take anything for granted. Be of service, do something that enriches somebody's life or helps the environment.

And most of all, believe in magic!

No exercises today, now it's up to you to choose whether or not you'd like to continue. Maybe you want to develop your own practices or maybe you need a break. I for myself will continue to create a magical life and I hope I've inspired you to do the same.

About the author

Flavia Waas has always been passionate about words. Writing is her favourite way of expressing herself and this book has been brewing inside of her for years. Her aim is to help other people to live an inspired life and "Magical May" is her first practical guide to doing so.

Printed in the United States
By Bookmasters